Umbrella Guide to
Alaska's Wilderness Highway

by
Mike Jensen

UMBRELLA
BOOKS
®

An imprint of Epicenter Press

Editor: J. Stephen Lay
Cover design: Elizabeth Watson
Cover photo: George Herben/Alaska Stock Images
Photos: School of Agriculture and Land Resources Management,
    University of Alaska Fairbanks
Maps: Scott Penwell
Pre-press production: Newman Design/Illustration, J. Stephen Lay
Printer: McNaughton & Gunn

© 1994 Mike Jensen
ISBN 0-945397-28-3
Library of Congress Catalog Card Number: 94-094292

To order single copies of
**UMBRELLA GUIDE TO
ALASKA'S WILDERNESS HIGHWAY**
send $10.95 (Washington residents add $.90 state sales tax)
plus $2 for book rate shipping to Epicenter Press,
Box 82368, Kenmore Station, Seattle, WA 98028.
Ask for our catalog. BOOKSELLERS: Retail discounts are available
from our trade distributor, Graphic Arts Center Publishing Co.,
Portland, OR. Call 800-452-3032.

PRINTED IN THE UNITED STATES OF AMERICA
First printing, June 1994
10 9 8 7 6 5 4 3 2 1

DEDICATION

To my father, Vern S. Jensen, who would have loved
Alaska and the Dalton region the way I do.

ACKNOWLEDGMENTS

Putting this guide together has been one of the most rewarding, interesting, and downright fun experiences I've ever had. I owe a great debt to a number of people who helped make this project such an enjoyable experience for me, and without whose help it would never have come about.

My thanks to John Murray, who gave me the idea for this guide and who helped me get oriented in the right direction. I also thank Joan Worley and Eric Heyne for their guidance and suggestions.

I could have never gotten past the planning stages of this guide without the help of representatives from several government agencies. My thanks to Roger Delaney and Jim Sisk of the Bureau of Land Management for introducing me to the Dalton region and opening their files for my use. I also thank Bob Hunter and Bill Avery of the Alaska Department of Fish and Game for teaching me about wildlife habitat and recreational opportunities in the Dalton region. Tom Edgerton, Anne-Marie Rizzi, and David Wiswar of the U.S. Fish and Wildlife Service gave me enough reading to last a lifetime on wildlife refuges and national parks. The Alaska State Troopers and the Department of Transportation and Public Facilities provided me with the travel and safety information so crucial to Dalton Highway visitors. Chris Marsh of the DOT was especially helpful.

I thank the University of Alaska Museum in Fairbanks for providing me with much-needed information on Dalton Highway history, plant life, and geology. University of Alaska Fairbanks professors Mike Gaffney and Eric Heyne supplied me with details on Dalton Highway history, and more importantly, helped me understand the meaning of that history. The National Weather Service was indispensable in helping me put together the *Climate* section of the guide.

I thank Lael Morgan, B.G. Olson, and Kent Sturgis for having the faith in both the subject matter and me to put this guide together. Thanks to Stephen Lay for his editorial work, and to Dr. John Fox, Will Lentz, Brett Carlson, Harry Bader, Dr. Don Triplehorn, and several officials of the BLM for their reviews. A special thanks to Pete Salzer and Alex Boyd, who spent more hours on the Dalton Highway with me than any of us cares to remember. And thanks to Nancy Schoephoester and Arco Alaska, Inc. for showing me the Prudhoe Bay oil fields and teaching me about oil production in the Alaskan arctic.

My greatest appreciation must go to my family. My study of the Dalton Highway can best be described as a passion bordering on obsession. I spent long hours doing research at government agencies, libraries, the University of Alaska Museum, and on the highway itself, and never once did I heard a single complaint. On the contrary, my family supported and sustained me, even pushed me to improve the manuscript, throughout the duration of the project. I thank Kandy, Christopher, Adam, and David for their patience and love.

Mike Jensen
Orem, Utah
April 5, 1994

PREFACE

In almost four decades of traveling the Far North, I've never met anyone as dedicated to it as James Dalton. Perhaps it was in his blood. His father was the illustrious Jack Dalton of Klondike Gold Rush fame. A tough man, rumored to have gunned down several opponents in cold blood, Dalton Sr. is thought to have arrived in the Alaskan arctic in about 1882. In 1890 he was hired to guide Edward J. Glave and A. B. Schanz, who had been engaged by *Leslie's Illustrated Newspaper* of New York to explore the Chilkat River to its interior reaches in the Yukon Territory.

For hundreds of years, Indians in this area had used three secret trading routes through the treacherous St. Elias Mountain Range. Two— the Chilkat and the White Pass—had just been discovered. Dalton and Glave found the third, broader and less abrupt than the others with grassy valleys where stock could be grazed. It was this route that later became known as the "Dalton Trail," where Jack began accumulating his fortune, running cattle and freight to supply the Klondike gold miners.

Jim Dalton was born into affluence in Seattle, but soon moved to Cordova because his father had mining interests there. Still very young when his mother died, Jim was shuttled off to military school. Later, pretty much on his own, he became an engineer and then joined the U.S. Navy.

It was the Navy that brought Jim Dalton back to Alaska—to the arctic coast where he would essentially spend the rest of his life. Like his father, he became an explorer, not for "yellow" gold but for "black gold" (petroleum and gas) which was the wealth of his era.

Jim and his wife, Kathleen "Mike" Dalton, were the first Caucasian couple ever to be married in the Navy camp near the Inupiat Eskimo settlement of Barrow on the arctic coast. Mike also fell under the spell of the Far North but after their two children, George and Libby, were born, the couple established a home in Fairbanks which is where I came to know them well.

Jim Dalton was a handsome, solid man of medium build, rather like his famous father, but a gentle man, and—more surprisingly for the rugged, outdoor type he was—a scholar. There were few classics that Dalton had not read. Books were his passion. He read Gray and Thackery for fun and traveled the world via print on those long dark arctic nights that are down time for heavy equipment operators. But his first love—beyond his family—was the high arctic. He was hooked on her lure, intrigued by her beauty, totally smitten with her promise.

And the arctic Dalton so thoroughly explored, made good—not only for Jim but for all Alaskans who enjoy the bounty of the oil wealth she has produced for the state and the sanctity of her unique, pristine wilderness that remains untapped.

It is fitting, I think, that not only the Dalton Highway but the awesome mountain that stands sentinel to it high above the Arctic Circle have been named for Jim. And I hope you enjoy them, as he did.

Lael Morgan
Fairbanks, AK

TABLE OF CONTENTS

An Introduction to the Dalton

If you have purchased this guide in anticipation of traveling the Dalton Highway—which I hope is the case—you are about to embark on the journey of a lifetime. The Dalton Highway is, in my opinion, the most beautiful and awe-inspiring stretch of road anywhere. Nobody who travels it does so without being deeply affected by the stark, wild beauty. I envy your journey.

I have written this guide to help you get the very most out of your trip along the Dalton Highway. I hope you use it for all it's worth. Read this guide thoroughly before beginning your trip north. Use the suggestions in the *Travel* and *Recreation* sections to help you plan your trip. Mark the areas in the separate sections and in the *Travel Log* that you are most interested in, and keep a watchful eye out as you drive. Follow the log as you go along and read about the natural and human-made wonders you find. Don't just drive the Dalton Highway: experience it.

The Dalton Highway

The Dalton Highway begins just north of the town of Livengood, Alaska, about eighty-four miles north of Fairbanks. It continues to the Prudhoe Bay oil fields on the Arctic Ocean, about 415 miles to the north. The highway crosses a continental divide at Atigun Pass (Mile 246.8) and covers three major ecological regions: the forested subalpine region of Alaska's Interior, the mountainous Brooks Range, and the tundra-covered Arctic Coastal Plain, also called the North Slope.

1

The road is a twenty-eight-foot-wide, all-weather gravel highway managed by the Alaska Department of Transportation and Public Facilities. It was built in 154 days between April and September 1974, at a total cost of $370,000,000. Its primary use is as a supply route for the oil facilities at Prudhoe Bay. Nearly 100 large trucks travel the highway each day. The few population centers are found at Yukon Crossing (Mile 56), Coldfoot (Mile 175), Wiseman (Mile 188.6), and Deadhorse (Mile 414.9). Deadhorse was established just south of Prudhoe Bay to house oil field contractors and their employees.

The Dalton Highway ends as you enter Deadhorse, several miles south of the Arctic Ocean. The oil fields begin on the north end of town. To visit the oil fields, you must make arrangements in advance to get past the checkpoints. See *Traveling the Dalton Highway* for instructions on arranging a tour of the oil fields.

Few roads leave the Dalton Highway. The Bettles Winter Road (Mile 135.7) is an ice road leading to the community of Bettles, AK, and is only open in winter. When the snow melts it becomes a quagmire, impassable by automobile. The Wiseman Road (Mile 188.6) leads to the historic mining community of Wiseman. This road is in fair condition, but it is not maintained in winter. The state has airports under lease at Five Mile Camp (Mile 60.5), Pump Station No. 5 (Mile 137.1), Coldfoot (Mile 175), Dietrich Camp (Mile 209.3), Chandalar Camp (Mile 239.2), and Galbraith Lake (Mile 274.7). There are also airstrips at Old Man Camp (Mile 107), Toolik Lake (Mile 284.2), and the Happy Valley Construction Camp (334.4).

The Dalton crosses a number of significant waterways, including the Kanuti River, the South and Middle Forks of the Koyukuk River, Prospect Creek, Hess Creek, Disaster Creek, and of course the mighty Yukon River. Galbraith and Toolik Lakes sit along the highway's path. Visitors also get breathtaking views of such imposing mountains as Caribou, Cathedral, Sukakpak, Dillon, and Snowden, along with a number of unnamed peaks within the majestic Brooks Range.

The Highway Region

For the purposes of this travel guide, the Dalton Highway region is defined as the highway itself and the lands immediately adjacent to it. Although the Dalton Highway itself is state owned and maintained, the land surrounding it has a variety of owners. There are a few private holdings along the highway, and there are a number of mining claims in the Koyukuk River Valley near the old mining towns of Coldfoot and Wiseman. However, the majority of the land is publicly owned and is managed by the state and federal government.

In addition to the highway itself, the state of Alaska owns nearly all of the land near the Dalton south of the Yukon River (Mile 56) and north of Slope Mountain (Mile 302). The strip of federally controlled land between these two points is called the Utility Corridor. You will spend the great majority of your time on the road in this corridor.

The Utility Corridor is managed by the Bureau of Land Management (BLM). The corridor is six to twenty-four miles wide. The southern portion of the corridor sits between the Kanuti and Yukon Flats National Wildlife Refuges. The northern portion divides the Arctic National Wildlife Refuge from Gates of the Arctic National Park.

The Utility Corridor was established in conjunction with the Dalton Highway to provide a route for transporting equipment and supplies needed for the trans-Alaska pipeline. The BLM grants leases to the private companies that provide services within the Utility Corridor. These services are only available at Yukon Ventures (Mile 56) and Coldfoot (Mile 175).

As a Dalton Highway traveler, you will be able to go almost anywhere you want along the highway's path. Please do not trespass on private land, Alyeska facilities and access roads, or the pipeline right-of-way—a twenty-seven foot boundary on either side of the pipeline itself. The University of Alaska Biology Field Research Station (Mile 284.2) is also closed to the public. The rest of the region surrounding the highway is open to most recreational activities, and, except for the area within a few hundred feet of the highway, is largely untouched by humans.

The Trans-Alaska Pipeline

The trans-Alaska pipeline and the Prudhoe Bay and nearby oil fields are the result of years of exploration, engineering, and expense. They are also the sole reason for the Dalton Highway's existence. The majority of traffic on the road consists of pipeline maintenance vehicles and large trucks hauling equipment to and from the oil fields.

Alyeska Pipeline Service Co., a consortium of the seven oil companies with holdings in the Prudhoe Bay oil field, was formed in 1970 to build and maintain the trans-Alaska pipeline. The first pipe in "the line"—as the trans-Alaska pipeline is often called—was laid on March 27, 1975, following six years of intensive engineering design and environmental planning. Pipeline designers had to deal with several engineering nightmares. For example, how do you transport oil with a temperature of ninety to one-hundred-twenty degrees Fahrenheit through a region of continuously frozen soil (permafrost) without destroying the terrain—and thus the pipeline itself? How do you allow caribou and other animals to pass from one side of the pipeline to the other? How do you allow the pipe to expand and contract with the heat and cold of the surrounding air without buckling? And what about earthquakes?

To avoid melting the frozen ground, engineers built the pipeline aboveground on 78,000 H-shaped vertical support members (VSMs) in areas of unstable permafrost. The stilts of these VSMs are filled with a liquid that boils at a temperature below water's 32° Fahrenheit freezing point. As the heat from the oil spreads through the VSMs towards the ground, this liquid reacts. Before the temperature in the stilt can climb to a point where it would thaw the surrounding permafrost, the liquid boils, changing to a gas. This gas then rises, eventually reaching a set of cooling fins at the top of the stilt. It then releases the heat into the atmosphere. With the heat dissipated, the gas changes back into a liquid and drains back to the bottom of the stilt, where the process begins again. The temperature of the stilts never rises to a point where the permafrost is affected.

More than 420 miles of the 800-mile-long pipeline sit aboveground. The 380 miles of buried pipe rest in areas where permafrost does not dominate. Because of external dangers, a few sections of the line had to be buried in permafrost-rich soil. For example, the pipeline was buried at permafrost-rich Atigun Pass where the risk of avalanche was too great to leave the line exposed. In these sections, the buried pipeline is heavily insulated to protect the surrounding soil.

In addition to protecting the terrain and the pipeline, the VSMs also raise the line to a minimum height of five feet aboveground, allowing for the unrestricted movement of caribou and other animals. Engineers also included several hundred sag-bend game crossings, which raise the pipe to over ten feet to allow animals to cross. Animals also cross over buried sections of pipe.

Another important feature of the VSMs is that they allow the pipeline to expand and contract with changes in the outside temperature. Most exposed sections of the line were built in a zig-zag pattern. When outside temperatures rise and the pipe expands, this zig-zag pattern creates an accordion effect. Instead of buckling, the pipeline moves horizontally along the VSMs. When outside temperatures cool and the pipe contracts, the same effect occurs. This allowance also helps protect the line from the effects of earthquakes. The pipeline system should be able to withstand an earthquake of magnitude 8.5 on the Richter Scale.

The final weld on the trans-Alaska pipeline was made near Pump Station 3 (Mile 311.9) on May 31, 1977, completing one of the greatest engineering feats of our time. The entire project cost more than $8 billion. The four-foot-diameter pipe went on-line on June 20 of that year. Oil from the pipeline reached Valdez harbor on July 28. On August 1, 1977, the first tanker filled with Prudhoe Bay oil left Valdez.

Over its 800-mile path from Prudhoe Bay to Valdez harbor—the northernmost ice-free port in North America—the trans-Alaska pipeline crosses thirteen major rivers and three mountain ranges. The line can move up to 2 million barrels of oil per day at an average speed of 6.25 miles per hour. It takes about five and one half days for the oil to travel from Prudhoe Bay to Valdez.

The trans-Alaska pipeline is maintained by several hundred Alyeska employees stationed in Anchorage, Fairbanks, Valdez, and at the ten pump stations along the pipeline route. In addition, hundreds of contractors help maintain the pipeline. The pipeline's Operations Control Center, located at Marine Terminal in Valdez, monitors the pipeline twenty-four hours a day. With Alyeska's monitoring and repair program, the pipeline is expected to last indefinitely.

The Oil Fields

The Prudhoe Bay oil field is the largest in North America. ARCO Alaska, Inc. operates the eastern half of this field, and BP Exploration operates the western half. Other significant fields, including the Kuparuk River oil field, the second-largest producing oil field in the U.S., and the Lisburne and Point McIntyre fields, have also been discovered in recent years. The expected total recoverable reserves from the Prudhoe Bay oil field is nearly 12 billion barrels of oil and 26 trillion cubic feet of natural gas. The Kuparuk field is expected to yield about 1.8 billion barrels of oil, and the other fields are expected to yield about 300 million barrels.

The oil fields around Prudhoe Bay are unlike any that most Dalton Highway travelers have seen. To begin with, the large mechanical pumps common on most U.S. oil fields do not exist at Prudhoe Bay. The field has a natural pressure that forces oil to the surface. ARCO and BP Exploration have used several methods, such as injecting water and natural gas into the wells as the oil is removed, to maintain that pressure. A wellhead observed on the surface is a collection of valves and fittings—called a "Christmas tree"—that controls the flow of oil and gas to and from the well. Up to forty wells are drilled on a single drill pad. Through directional drilling, these forty wells can drill for six square miles beneath the earth's surface.

Another interesting difference between the North Slope oil fields and other U.S. fields is their foundation. Just about everything at Prudhoe Bay—including the town of Deadhorse—is build on a six-foot-thick gravel pad. A layer of insulating foam is imbedded in the pad, which keeps the ground frozen and stable. All buildings at Prudhoe Bay are set on gravel pads or pilings, or both. The gravel for these pads is taken from the Prudhoe Bay area itself.

The oil companies have come up with an ingenious use for their old gravel pits. Most waterways on the North Slope freeze solid in the winter, making it impossible for fish to thrive. However, these old gravel pits are deep enough that they don't freeze to the bottom when filled with water. So that's what the oil companies do. The empty pits are filled with water, and fish are introduced into the new pond. The following summer, many of these fish are moved to area rivers and streams. Thus, anglers can fish many waterways that normally would not support fish.

All North Slope oil field workers are housed at Prudhoe Bay. Both ARCO and BP Exploration have constructed operations centers and living quarters for their employees, who work twelve-hour shifts, seven days on and seven days off. The living quarters provide personal rooms, a dining room and snack bars, a movie theater, a library, a medical facility, game rooms, and exercise space and equipment, including inside basketball courts. BP even has a small swimming pool—which doubles as a holding tank for their fire suppression system.

On the Dalton

Keeping the Dalton Highway region a pristine wilderness is an important goal of the oil companies and the federal and state agencies responsible for the region. In an attempt to preserve the natural wilderness, several government agencies, along with researchers from the University of Alaska Fairbanks and with the cooperation of the Prudhoe Bay oil companies, conduct extensive research in the area. These researchers continually study the impact of the oil fields, the trans-Alaska pipeline, and the Dalton Highway on the wildlife and vegetation. Their ongoing research is invaluable in allowing travelers to have the Dalton experience in its purest form.

History

Humans have a long and rich history in the Dalton Highway region. From the beginning of this history until the present, the relationship between humankind and the area has been one of exploration, discovery, and adaptation. From the first humans to set foot in the region to those who now live, work, and play there, the inhabitants of the region have come to respect and appreciate this harsh and forbidding land.

The First Alaskans

According to scientists, during the Pleistocene Ice Age—about 12,000 years ago—much of the water covering the earth's surface was frozen. Ocean levels around the globe lowered as water froze into glacial ice. This lowering of ocean levels exposed continental shelves and other land masses that had previously been covered by water. One of these exposed continental shelves stretched between Asia and North America, forming a 600-mile-wide bridge between the two continents. This bridge, known today as the Bering Land Bridge, allowed plants and animals to migrate from what is today Siberia, Russia, to Alaska. Many anthropologists believe that the bridge also allowed the nomadic ancestors of today's Alaska Natives to follow this migratory path.

According to anthropologists, several groups crossed the Bering Land Bridge during the Pleistocene Ice Age. Upon reaching this new continent, they spread throughout North America. Some groups settled in the southern regions of what is now Alaska, from Sitka to the end of the Aleutian island chain. The descendants of these groups include the Tlingit, Tsimshian, and Haida Indians and the Aleuts.

One of the early groups across the bridge became the forerunners of today's Athabascan Indians. This group settled throughout the Interior of present-day Alaska and in sections of Canada's Yukon Territory, Northwest Territories, and British Columbia. Athabascan dialects are even present in the languages of the Navajo and Apache Indians. The group that settled the Dalton Highway region of Alaska's Interior were the ancestors of today's Koyukon Athabascans, one of twelve major Athabascan sub-groups.

The other primary settlers of the Dalton region did not arrive in Alaska until long after the Interior had been settled. About 4,000-5,000 years ago, another land bridge crossing brought a large group of inhabitants to North America. This group spread throughout the arctic rim, from Alaska to Greenland. Those that settled in the region stayed north of the Brooks Range and are the ancestors of today's Inupiaq Eskimos.

The first Alaska inhabitants faced harsh living conditions. The climate was severe and the land inhospitable. In spite of these conditions, however, these peoples developed a unique and complex culture and left a wealth of information about themselves. There are several known archeological sites in the Dalton region, and the University of Alaska Museum in Fairbanks has a wonderful collection of artifacts from the area.

The early Alaska settlers were accomplished hunters. The pre-Athabascans of the Interior often followed herds of caribou for hundreds of miles in order to collect enough meat to last the winter. Further north, the pre-Inupiaq also followed the great herds of caribou that migrated across the tundra. They also hunted walrus, seals, and polar bears. Daring Eskimo hunters harpooned whales from small, skin-covered boats called "umiaks."

European Explorers

The ancestors of today's Athabascans and Eskimos lived for thousands of years in what we now call Alaska before the first Europeans set foot on the continent. The first Europeans to reach Alaska were the Russians. On July 16, 1741, Vitus Bering, a Danish sea captain who sailed under the Russian flag, first sighted the Alaska mainland and claimed it for the czar. Bering died while returning to Asia that December, but a flood of explorers—destined to change Alaska forever—had just begun.

Early explorers were too occupied surveying and mapping the western and southern coasts of Alaska to explore inland to the Dalton region. The Russians sent Alexis Chirikof, who explored Sitka harbor and the Aleutian Islands in 1741. The English sent Captain James Cook, who explored Southeast Alaska and named many of the areas in that region—Prince William Sound, Cook Inlet—in 1778. Spain, France, and even the newly formed United States of America sent explorers to this new region.

Traders and Prospectors

The Eskimos and Athabascans deep within the Alaska mainland felt little impact from this early exploration of the coast. As the Russians took control of Alaska and began the massive harvest of sea otter furs, the Dalton region remained much the same as it had for centuries. But the Europeans did not leave the region alone forever, however. In 1845, John Bell of the Hudson's Bay Company reached the Yukon Flats and discovered a wealth of beaver, otter, muskrat, marten, mink, lynx, weasel, wolverine, fox, and wolf. Two years later, Fort Yukon was established on the Yukon River, making it the first English-speaking community in Interior Alaska.

In 1880, just thirteen years after the U.S. took ownership of Alaska, Richard Harris and Joe Juneau discovered the mineral that forever changed Alaska, especially the Dalton region: gold. The two prospectors found the mineral near present day Juneau, named for Joe, and soon prospectors began pouring into Alaska. In 1896, gold was discovered on the Klondike River in Canada's Yukon Territory. More than 100,000 fortune-seekers headed for the Klondike gold fields. Gold was discovered in Nome in 1898, and within two years 18,000 prospectors had arrived in that city.

Soon discoveries were being made in the Dalton region. In 1899, gold was discovered in many of the creeks around present-day Coldfoot, and in 1902 Felix Pedro and Tom Gilmore discovered gold just north of Fairbanks. By 1903 mining communities had sprung up at Fox, Olnes, Gilmore, and Chatanika. The Tanana Valley Mines Railroad was built in 1905 to haul freight from the town of Chena, which sat on the Tanana River and received goods from river boats, to these camps.

In 1908 gold was discovered near Wiseman, and many prospectors abandoned other areas of Alaska. In 1914, Jay Livengood and N. R. Hudson discovered gold near what is now the town of Livengood, the starting point of the Dalton Highway. The Elliott Highway, which leads from just north of Fairbanks to Mile 0 of the Dalton, began as a fifty-two-mile sled road used to haul supplies between the camps of Olnes and Livengood. Prospectors, merchants, and other settlers were now firmly entrenched in what for thousands of years had been Eskimo and Indian lands.

Wealth, Exploration, and War

Several factors played a part in the continued development of the Dalton region. The great wealth of this vast U.S. property to the north caught the attention of the U.S. government, which granted Alaska territorial status in 1912. The development of Alaska's mineral resources became a top priority of the new territory. In 1917 the Alaska Agricultural College and School of Mines, now the University of Alaska Fairbanks, was established in part to further mineral exploration.

In 1923 the Alaska Railroad was formally opened, bringing mass transit to Alaska's Interior. In 1924, Carl Ben Eielson demonstrated the feasibility of air travel in the region by successfully flying deep into the Interior from Fairbanks. This opened up areas of Alaska previously inaccessible to travel or exploration. In the late 1920s and throughout the 1930s, forester Robert Marshall lived among the people of the Dalton region and explored much of the territory. His maps of the northern Koyukuk region displayed nearly 150 new names, many of which had been used for years but were unknown outside the region. Marshall also named several landscape features himself (see Miles 205, 227.3 in the *Travel Log*). Gates of the Arctic National Park took its name from Marshall's description of two Brooks Range peaks, Frigid Crags and Boreal Mountain. Marshall eventually wrote two books, *Arctic Village* and *Alaska Wilderness*, about the region, opening it up to anyone who could read.

During World War II, Alaska was recognized for its strategic military position in the Pacific. In 1942 the U.S. Army built the Alaska Highway from Dawson Creek, British Columbia in Canada to Delta Junction, about 100 miles south of Fairbanks. Even today the Alaska Highway provides the only overland access to the Dalton Highway region from outside the state of Alaska, and is the most popular route to the Dalton for out-of-state travelers.

Oil and the Highway

The discovery of the multi-billion-barrel oil reserve at Prudhoe Bay in 1968 changed the Dalton Highway area more than any other event since gold was found in the Interior. The $900 million Prudhoe Bay lease sale allowing the oil companies to drill for the oil provided the resources necessary to modernize public services throughout Alaska. The Alaska Native Claims Settlement Act of 1971, which granted the pipeline a clear right-of-way through the state, provided lands and money to a number of newly created Native corporations.

Immediately after oil was discovered by the Atlantic-Richfield Co. (ARCO), a winter ice road was constructed from Livengood to the oil fields. This first road was a bulldozer-bladed trail over which trucks and "cat trains"—caterpiller tractors pulling two or three sleds—drove on the exposed frozen ground and crossed streams on ice bridges. It was named "the Hickel Highway" after then-governor Walter Hickel.

The trans-Alaska pipeline and the Dalton Highway cross dozens of streams and rivers in their passage north.

The Hickel Highway traversed the Yukon River about seven miles upstream of the current bridge, crossed the Yukon and Kanuti Flats, and then intersected today's Dalton Highway just north of Fish Creek (Mile 114). It then turned west to Bettles, continued up the John River through Anaktuvuk Pass in the Brooks Range, and followed west of the Sagavanirktok River to Prudhoe Bay. The Hickel Highway was usually a driver's nightmare, and was only accessible for a few months every winter.

In August 1969 construction began on a new, more permanent road between Livengood and Prudhoe Bay. The new highway was constructed in two sections. The first section, built between August 1969 and July 1970, extended approximately fifty-six miles from Livengood to the Yukon River. This section was referred to as the TAPS (trans-Alaska pipeline system) Road. After environmental reviews and delays to settle land claims of Alaska Natives, the second section, the 358-mile-long Haul Road between the Yukon River and Prudhoe Bay, was built between April 29 and September 29, 1974. Ten temporary construction camps and several airfields were built along the way.

In 1981 the Haul Road was renamed "the Dalton Highway" in honor of James William Dalton. James Dalton (1913-1977) was a pioneer of arctic oil exploration. He received a degree in mining engineering from the University of Alaska in 1937. After short stints in the gold-mining industry and the U.S. Navy Seabees—the construction arm of the Navy—he began his oil exploration career in the Alaskan arctic.

In 1946, Dalton accepted a position as foreman with Arctic Contractors, an organization involved in oil and gas exploration in Naval Petroleum Reserve No. 4 on the Arctic Coastal Plain of Alaska. He worked for Arctic Contractors until their exploration work was suspended in 1953. He was the general superintendent of the company for the last year and a half of their operations, and in this capacity supervised all operations in the arctic region.

From 1955 to 1957 he was the assistant project manager of the Alaskan section of the DEW (Distant Early Warning) Line, a radar system constructed from Thule, Greenland, across Canada, and across Alaska under direction of the U.S. Department of Defense.

When he finished his work on the DEW line, Dalton resumed his work with the Navy as a consultant for the Director of the Naval Petroleum and Oil Shale Reserves. From 1957 to 1975, he supervised mineral and petroleum exploration throughout Alaska, including sites around the Alaska Peninsula and Cook Inlet. Much of his work, however, was still centered in the Arctic Coastal Plain, including extensive work at Prudhoe Bay and Barrow. Dalton was instrumental in choosing the location where the giant Prudhoe Bay oil reserve was discovered. Jim Dalton died May 9, 1977, twenty-two days before the final weld was completed on the trans-Alaska pipeline.

The Dalton Highway Region Today

When the trans-Alaska pipeline was finished in 1977, the Dalton region became primarily a commercial corridor for the transportation of goods to and from the Prudhoe Bay oil fields. However, in 1981 the State of Alaska opened the highway to the public as far as Disaster Creek (Mile 210.5), and private use has steadily increased since that time. The region has also become a popular recreational area. Bow hunters, anglers, backpackers, and boaters all travel up the highway in ever-increasing numbers to enjoy the beauty and activities of the area.

Climate

Because the Dalton region encompasses such a wide area, the climate varies considerably over the course of the highway. The region can be divided into two distinct climatic zones: the Interior Zone and the Arctic Zone. The Interior Zone includes that portion of the Dalton region from Livengood to the Continental Divide (Atigun Pass, Mile 246.8). The Arctic Zone includes everything north of the divide.

The Interior is a region of temperature extremes and relatively low precipitation. Temperatures in the Interior can span more than a 150-degree range, from winter lows in excess of -60° F to summer highs of 90°F or more. Averages, however (-5° F to -25° F in winter and 60° F to 70° F in summer) are more tolerable.

The lowlands and river bottoms of the Interior experience the most dramatic temperature swings, while the mountains "rise above" these extremes. In the summer, the mountains stay cooler because they are higher in elevation. In winter they stay warmer because of the effects of inversions.

Inversions are caused when cold, heavy air settles to the valley floors and becomes trapped as warmer, lighter air passes above it. The valleys experience extremely cold temperatures from the trapped cold air, while the mountains remain in the warmer air above. The all-time official low temperature recorded in the state, -80° F, was recorded during an inversion at Prospect Creek (Mile 135.2) in 1971.

The Interior Zone receives from ten to thirteen inches of precipitation each year. Most of this moisture comes during the summer, when powerful thunderstorms pass through the region from the south or southwest. During the winter, cold, dry air dominates the Interior. Occasionally moist air will enter the region from the west or southwest coast, causing major snowstorms. The Interior usually receives from fifty to seventy inches of snow each winter. However, because of its extreme dryness, this snow accounts for little actual precipitation.

The Arctic Zone is a region of low temperatures and precipitation. Winter lows of -60° F in the Arctic Zone are about equal to those in the Interior. However, summer highs rarely exceed 60° F due to the influence of the Arctic Ocean. During the summer, a cool sea breeze blows in from the ocean. This breeze brings with it lower temperatures and morning coastal fog that can reach nearly thirty miles inland, often reaching Franklin Bluffs (Mile 391.2).

The Arctic Zone gets only four to five inches of precipitation each year. The intense thunderstorms of the Interior are much less common beyond Atigun Pass. Most North Slope precipitation comes in the form of frequent, light rain and snow showers blowing in from the Arctic Ocean.

The Arctic Zone is greatly affected by wind throughout much of the year. Unlike the Interior, where the hilly terrain effectively blocks most wind, the flat Coastal Plain allows sea breezes to sweep unblocked across the region. These breezes are not usually strong. They average only about twelve miles per hour, but they are almost always present and can reach thirty to fifty miles per hour or more. These breezes can cause heavy snow drifts, poor visibility, and wind-chill factors in excess of -100° F.

Winter throughout the entire Dalton Highway region is long and harsh. The first snowfall usually occurs in the northern end of the region by early- to mid-August, and the snow stays on the ground well into May and even June. Most visitors only travel the highway during a 120-day travel season (see *Traveling the Dalton Highway*). Even during this travel season, however, the weather can change very quickly from inviting to inclement. Be prepared for a wide range of weather conditions. The following gives a rough summary of the weather you are likely to encounter on the highway during the travel season. To get current weather information before you begin your trip, call the National Weather Service and get an area forecast (see *Index of Agencies*).

May

The Dalton region is just coming to life when the first visitors venture onto the highway in mid-May. Temperatures have been above freezing for about a month south of the Brooks Range, and breakup has already occurred. Daytime temperatures range from the low forties to mid-fifties, and nighttime lows are near freezing. The snow is usually gone or melting quickly in the Interior, although fields linger at several places.

The Arctic Zone is still largely held in winter's grasp during the month. Daytime highs only reach into the mid-thirties, and several days do not break above freezing. Nighttime lows are in single digits or the teens. The Arctic Zone experiences almost no precipitation during May.

June

Daily highs in the Interior run in the high sixties and low seventies in June, and some days may reach the eighties. Lows are usually in the forties, although some June nights drop below freezing. Thunderstorm activity in the Interior begins in late June, and you should expect some poor weather during this month.

North of Atigun Pass, breakup is just beginning near the end of the month. Highs break into the forties for the first time, and will range from 40° Fahrenheit to 60° Fahrenheit. Lows will be in the thirties or lower. The Arctic Zone receives very little precipitation in June. What does come is usually in the form of light rain showers.

July

July is the Interior's hottest and wettest month. Temperatures average in the sixties and seventies, and you will probably experience a few days in the high 80s and even the 90s. Lows will be in the high forties and low fifties. Thunderstorm activity is in full swing, dropping more than two inches of precipitation in the region during the month.

July is also the Arctic Zone's warmest month. Breakup is complete by mid-July, and plant and animal life is suddenly abundant. Daily highs move into the high fifties, and lows are usually in the mid- to high-30s. Arctic storm activity increases slightly in July, with weak, low-pressure fronts moving into the region from the west. By July the temperature is warm enough to move the sea ice away from the shores around the oil fields.

August

August brings a cooling trend to the Interior Zone, as daily highs drop back to the high fifties and low sixties—although seventies and eighties are still frequent. Lows drop to the high thirties and low forties. Thunderstorms are less common in August, and are replaced by day-long drizzles as the month draws to a close.

North of Atigun Pass, high temperatures move to the forties, with low temperatures in the low- to mid-30s. Nighttime lows regularly drop below freezing. Rainfall peaks in the Arctic Zone this month, with several mild storms moving through. These numerous storms leave nearly twenty-five percent of the region's total annual precipitation.

September

Freezeup is well underway throughout the Dalton region by September. Daytime highs in the Interior rarely exceed 50° Fahrenheit and lows fall below freezing almost every night. Summer thunderstorms have ended, and any precipitation during this month usually comes in the form of snow showers that move in from the west coast.

In the Arctic Zone, daytime highs rarely exceed freezing, with lows in the teens and twenties. Small ponds and lakes have frozen for the year, and vegetation is dormant once again—and covered with snow.

Terrain

According to geologists, this immense landmass that we call Alaska did not exist—at least not in one piece—until about 200 million years ago. The bits of oceanic crust and continental sediment that would one day become Alaska were still on their way here. At that time, North America's west coast lay somewhere along the western edge of the Canadian Rockies.

At about 200 million years ago, mudstone, sandstone, and shale began to gather along North America's west coast after a long journey across the Pacific Ocean. A combination of pressure, heat, and water caused these ancient—up to 1 billion years old—rocks to undergo a physical change, or "metamorphosis." They picked up minerals, such as quartz, that gathered in streaks or plates in the rocks. This is the same process that allows gold to form in veins in surrounding rock. This metamorphic rock began to build up along the North American west coast, extending the coast further to the west.

In the northernmost regions of the Canadian Rockies, this metamorphic rock began spreading into what we now call Interior Alaska. This first Alaskan terrain is called the Yukon Tanana Uplands, and it acted like a skeletal foundation for the rest of the state to build upon. The Yukon-Tanana terrain underlies most of the landscape leading to Mile 0 of the Dalton Highway, including the city of Fairbanks and all of the Steese Expressway and Elliott Highway.

As you drive from Fairbanks to the Dalton Highway, you will immediately recognize the main characteristic of the Yukon Tanana Uplands: the deeply eroded hills. This terrain is known for rounded hills separated by low-lying streams and river basins.

What we now call the Dalton region was formed directly around this oldest section of Alaska. The Dalton region south of the Brooks Range was formed as more oceanic crust and sediment migrated up the west coast and became connected to the Yukon Tanana Uplands. The northern region came a different route. This terrain joined Alaska when an oceanic plate to the north began to move south towards the new territory. This plate eventually ran up against what was then northern Alaska. As the two plates ground against each other over thousands of years, the Brooks Range was born. The northern edge of this plate became the new northern Alaska coast.

Geologically, the Dalton Highway region is considered part of the Western Cordillera system, a wide, mountainous belt of land that stretches from Central America through the Rocky Mountains of the forty-eight contiguous United States and Canada to Alaska. Within the Dalton region, the cordillera is separated into four very distinct types of land-scape: the Tozitna terrain, the Ruby terrain, the Brooks Range terrain, and the Arctic Coastal Plain (or North Slope) terrain.

Tozitna Terrain

From Mile 0 of the Dalton to the Yukon River (Mile 55.5), the Dalton passes over what is called the Tozitna terrain. This terrain is very similar to the Yukon-Tanana terrain to which it is connected. The Tozitna terrain is marked by relatively low, rounded hills (300 to 3,200 feet) of ancient metamorphic rock over 500 million years old. This rock is mostly schist with some outcroppings of basalt, sandstone, and lime-stone. Most Tozitna rock is hidden beneath a covering of frozen "loess"—silt carried by the wind from glacial stream beds.

Ruby Terrain

From just north of the Yukon River until about Coldfoot (Mile

Three visitors climb among the rocks on Finger Mountain. This tor, just a few feet off the highway, offers visitors the best opportunity to explore a tor along the Dalton Highway.

175), the highway passes over the Ruby terrain. This terrain marks a fairly drastic shift from the rolling hills of the Yukon-Tanana and Tozitna landscape. The Ruby terrain consists primarily of schist, greenstone, and gneiss. Greenstone is an igneous rock that has picked up green minerals as it metamorphosed. Gneiss is similar to schist, with striped bands of light and dark minerals.

An interesting characteristic of the Ruby terrain is the granite that underlies the metamorphic rock. This exceptionally solid rock causes some interesting landscape features to develop.

Tors

Tors are granite rock pinnacles that survive as less-resistant metamorphic rock erodes around them over centuries. You will see several tors between Mile 56 and about Mile 150 of the Dalton Highway. Finger Rock (Mile 97.5), standing near the summit of Finger Mountain, is the best known tor along the Dalton route. Another tor on Finger Mountain sits within a few feet of the highway and lets travelers get a close-up view of this phenomenon.

Sandy Domes

Several hills between the Yukon River and Coldfoot have granite foundations. These hills are referred to as "sandy domes." Sand Hill (Mile 73) is a sandy dome, and Old Man Camp (Mile 107) is built on one. These granite-based hills are similar in their makeup to Stone Mountain in Georgia. If you were to get out of your car and do a little exploring on one of these sandy domes, you would find course sand on the ground. This sand is formed as frost action belowground grinds and crushes the underlying granite. Some sand eventually works its way to the surface, and thus we get sandy domes.

The Brooks Range

The landscape between Coldfoot and Galbraith Lake (Mile 272.5) has a unique geologic history. In the first few miles between Coldfoot and Wiseman (Mile 188.6), the terrain is made of 500 million-year-old metamorphic rock, such as greenstone and quartzite. But at Wiseman the terrain changes drastically. Before the Brooks and Alaska Ranges were uplifted, the Yukon Tanana Uplands had the highest elevation in the state. The area between Wiseman and Galbraith Lake was a lowland basin, and was often covered by great bodies of water.

Because of this, the terrain between Wiseman and Galbraith Lake is composed of sedimentary instead of metamorphic rock. In other words, the terrain is made of organic and inorganic matter that was deposited on the sea floor by ocean currents. Sandstone, shale, and limestone accumulated in great amounts in this region.

When the Brooks Range was forced upwards, this sea floor became mountainous terrain. This causes an interesting phenomenon in the region. The South Fork Koyukuk River (Mile 156.1), which is glacially fed, is aquamarine in color, much like the waters of the Caribbean. The reason for this is the limestone in the Brooks Range. As glaciers grow in the Brooks Range, they pick up bits of sedimentary limestone from what used to be the sea floor. When they recede, the limestone deposits are released into the stream flow, turning the water aquamarine.

Glaciers

Although usually thought of in terms of past ice ages, glaciers are very much a part of the present in the Dalton region. Although few glaciers can be seen directly from the road (see Mile 274.7 of the *Travel Log*), dozens of them persist in the Brooks Range. Several rivers and streams south of the range are at least partially fed by glacial runoff.

Glaciers are large masses of snow and ice that persist in an area for many years. They are formed when more snow falls than melts in an area. Eventually this snow is compressed into dense ice and begins to "move," or grow, with the added snow. Glaciers continue to grow until they reach a point at which snow melt equals snowfall, and they stop. If temperatures rise in a glacial area, snow melt will surpass snowfall, and glaciers will "recede," or melt back towards their origin.

Scientists believe that the last period of major glacial advance on the earth was during the Wisconsinan Glaciation. This glaciation reached

As ice in the ground expands, it has nowhere to go but up. The force of the expanding ice alters the surface terrain in numerous ways including pingos, thaw lakes, and polygons.

its peak about 18,000 years ago, during the Pleistocene Ice Age. During this period, several glaciers moved as far south as Grayling Lake (Mile 150.3). As these glaciers receded, they left specific landscape features as distinct as fingerprints marking their presence.

The most obvious and widespread post-glacial features along the Dalton Highway are the U-shaped valleys common from Grayling Lake north. Because rivers are relatively thin bands of cutting material, valleys carved by rivers are V-shaped and have narrow valley floors. Glaciers have very wide bases and steep sides, thus forming broad, steep, U-shaped valleys.

Sometimes the right conditions can cause river valleys to look like glacially formed valleys. For example, several valleys between Fairbanks and Grayling Lake have broad floors. These valleys were carved by rivers, however, as this area has never been glaciated. At one time they had a normal, V-shaped appearance. However, when the Alaska Range rose about 100 million years ago, it depressed the Yukon Tanana Uplands. The slope of the rivers were reduced and so was their ability to carry sediment. The Alaska Range also dumped between 150 and 200 feet of sediment into the Tanana basin. This sediment filled in the valley floors and made them appear broad and flat, like glacially carved valleys. If you'll notice, however, the valley walls still have the less steep, V-shaped appearance of river-formed valleys.

Another marker left by past glaciers is the landslide. While landslides can occur for many reasons, they are common in glaciated areas. The carving action of glaciers makes valley walls steeper than they normally would be. When glaciers recede, these artificially steep walls sometimes are unable to support their own surface matter. Eventually sections of the valley wall give way. Many of the landslides seen beyond Mile 150 are a result of glacial action.

The Arctic Coastal Plain

From about Galbraith Lake north to the Arctic Ocean is Alaska's Arctic Coastal Plain, or North Slope. The North Slope marks a drastic change from the 3,900- to 8,100-foot peaks of the Brooks Range.

Most of the terrain underlying this section of the Dalton region consists of sediments eroded from the Brooks Range. These sediments include shale, sandstone, and gravel. The vast oil reserves at Prudhoe Bay come from organically rich shale found in the northernmost reaches of this area. The gravel used to underlie almost everything in Deadhorse and at the oil fields also comes from these abundant sedimentary deposits.

The North Slope terrain can best be described in one word: flat. The southernmost portion of this terrain, the arctic foothills, boasts a few 600- to 3,500-foot buttes, knobs, and mesas as it emerges from the Brooks Range. But these land forms quickly diminish as the highway progresses north. The foothills—and any semblance of elevation—disappear completely near Pump Station No. 2 (Mile 358.8). For the last fifty-five miles or so, the highway descends the gentle slope of the Arctic Coastal Plain. From this point north, pingos provide the only break in the landscape.

Permafrost

Although permafrost is not a type of Dalton Highway terrain, it is by far the most dominant feature of the highway landscape. It is so prevalent in all the terrain of the Dalton region that it deserves its own section. Although you will probably never actually see permafrost, you will see its effects everywhere you look in the region. It determines to a great extent what plant life exists in the region, and it was the primary obstacle to overcome during construction of both the Dalton Highway and the trans-Alaska pipeline.

Permafrost is a layer of material that remains frozen for two or more years beneath the earth's surface. It may consist of soils, organic matter, and even bedrock. It usually contains large amounts of water. Permafrost underlies about twenty percent of the earth's surface and is the most widespread in the arctic. The permafrost is nearly 2,000 feet thick at certain spots along Alaska's Arctic Coastal Plain.

Permafrost forms when underground material freezes more deeply in the winter than it thaws in the summer. When this happens, a layer of permanently frozen ground—or "permafrost"—develops. If temperatures stay low enough for this ground to remain frozen, the permafrost grows downward until it is balanced by the heat flowing upward from the earth's interior.

Each summer, from several inches to several feet of the permafrost will thaw, but the lower levels will remain frozen. Thus, separate layers will form in the ground. The section of ground that thaws each summer is called the "active layer." The upper surface of the remaining permafrost is called the "permafrost table." The bottom surface of the permafrost is called the "base."

Occasionally, portions of unfrozen ground will develop between sections of permafrost. This usually happens when an unusually warm summer occurs, followed by a mild winter. For example, a warm summer may melt the active layer to a depth of three feet, and the following mild winter may only freeze the ground to a depth of two feet. The one foot of unfrozen ground caught between these two frozen sections is called "talik."

Ground ice is often a major ingredient—up to half the total volume—of permafrost. Ice may occur in individual grains; in veins like gold in a mountainside; as lenses in round or oblong chunks; or as ice wedges, which are shaped somewhat like downward-pointing ax heads.

Two different permafrost zones exist in the Dalton region: the continuous zone and the discontinuous zone. Where permafrost is continuous, there are no permafrost-free areas. North of Atigun Pass (Mile 246.8) is a continuous permafrost zone.

In discontinuous permafrost, areas with underlying permafrost are intermixed with permafrost-free areas. South of Atigun Pass is a discontinuous permafrost zone. The discontinuous permafrost zone stretches over much of the state of Alaska, reaching as far south as the Alaska Range just north of Anchorage.

Pingos

A number of unique landforms arise as a direct result of permafrost-rich soil. Pingos are cone-shaped hills that form over permafrost on the

Arctic Coastal Plain. Pingos range from 10 to 180 feet in height and can
be several thousand feet in diameter. They are formed when an underground spring freezes above permafrost. The water expands as it freezes,
and since the permafrost does not allow the water to expand downward,
it bows upward, lifting the soil with it. You will see several large
pingos as you near Deadhorse.

Ice-cored Mounds

Ice-cored mounds are similar to pingos, although they are much
smaller and can form and disappear in a few days. Ice-cored mounds
can occasionally be seen along the Dalton route south of the Brooks
Range. Sometimes ice-cored mounds will break open and the underlying ice can be seen.

Polygons

Polygons are extremely common on the Arctic Coastal Plain. In
polygons, the ground ice present in the permafrost forms in a honeycomb network. The ice-free centers of these networks often recede
slightly, so that observers can see the underlying honeycomb design.

Thaw Lakes

Thaw lakes often form when plant cover is removed from permafrost in wet, low-lying areas. Plant cover acts like insulation, so if the
plants are removed and the ground is exposed, the permafrost thaws,
the ground subsides, and water pools in the low spot. Thaw lakes
continue to grow as the accumulated water thaws additional permafrost
at its edges. Thaw lakes on the North Slope have a very distinctive
northwest-to-southeast directional slant because the breeze from the
Arctic Ocean blows pond currents in that direction.

The Permafrost Dilemma

Permafrost was a serious concern for the builders of the Dalton Highway and the trans-Alaska pipeline. To maintain a stable ground surface to support the road and the pipeline, engineers had to find a way to build without thawing the permafrost. To do this, they had to perform several engineering feats, including installing refrigeration units under the bases of the pump stations and buried sections of the pipeline; planting grasses under the pipeline to replace lost, insulating ground cover; designing the vertical support members to carry the pipeline; and using foam imbedded in gravel to insulate every human-made object constructed in the area. Although some initial problems developed, the road and pipeline have held fairly stable for a number of years, and have become interesting aspects of the terrain in their own rights.

Plants

The Dalton Highway region is home to numerous plant communities. From forests of spruce and aspen to moss-covered bogs to the tundra, plants forever highlight the land in a panorama of colors, textures, and patterns.

The two major ecological divisions represented along the highway are the boreal forest, or "taiga"—a Russian word meaning "land of little sticks"—and the tundra. In addition to trees and tundra, shrub communities are also found in some areas. From Livengood to treeline near the base of the Chandalar Shelf (Mile 235.3), forested areas dominate, interrupted occasionally by treeless bogs in the lowlands and alpine tundra above 2,500 feet. Arctic tundra is the dominant community on the Arctic Coastal Plain.

The growth rate of trees and shrubs in the Dalton Highway region is very slow. Because of the extremely short growing season, it may take 300 years for a white spruce at treeline to reach a diameter of five inches. Waist-high willows may be 50-100 years old. This is one reason why it is so important to protect the vegetation. Damage can take literally centuries to mend.

Several factors come into play in determining what plant communities will grow in different locations in the region. These factors include direction and steepness of mountain slope, drainage, elevation, permafrost levels, and fire history. South-facing mountain slopes will carry thicker, more vigorous vegetation than other terrain because the trees and shrubs on these slopes are exposed to much greater light and warmth than those in other areas.

As a general rule, steeper slopes will be home to more vigorous vegetation than other terrain. Soil drains better and thaws more quickly on steep slopes than it will on more gradual slopes or in river basins and other low-lying areas. However, extremely high elevation slopes can be devoid of forest communities altogether. Forested areas survive only to about 2,500 feet in the Dalton Highway region. At higher elevations temperatures are too extreme.

Permafrost levels affect the development of plant communities more than any other natural phenomenon. This frozen soil does not allow plant roots to grow deeply and gain a strong hold. Any penetration the roots get in the permafrost is of little use: Moisture is permanently frozen and the plants cannot absorb nutrients in the extreme cold. Additionally, permafrost flourishes in the worst areas for plant growth— gradual north-facing slopes and low-lying areas. Plants in these areas have to overcome the disadvantages of low light, cool temperatures, and poor drainage in addition to the challenges posed by the frozen ground.

Where permafrost is absent, trees flourish. Along riverbanks, moving water keeps the surrounding ground thawed, allowing more vigorous trees to grow. In several locations along the Dalton Highway, low-lying bogs contain few trees except along the riverbanks, where trees are able to thrive.

Fire affects plant communities in two important ways. As a fire passes through a forest, it clears out old, unproductive vegetation. When forests reach 150-300 years of age, they may become dominated by black spruce. Not only is black spruce a poor source of food for most wildlife, it also chokes off other, more productive food sources, such as herbs, shrubs, and willows. Consequently, mature forests no longer provide adequate food for many animal species.

Several hundred thousand acres of forest land burn each year in Alaska. When fire passes through an over-mature forest, everything, including the dense spruce cover, is burned off. As the forest recovers, the first plants to grow back are the herbs, shrubs, and willows. They return almost immediately after the fire and provide food for wildlife. It takes several years before spruce again dominates.

Fire can also affect plant communities by changing the underlying terrain. When a fire passes through a forest on permafrost-rich soil, the heat of the fire, combined with the loss of shade and insulating organic matter on the forest floor, may cause the underlying permafrost to thaw. Until the permafrost can become reestablished—a process that can take decades—the new forest will grow vigorously, just like those forests on permafrost-free areas.

Forests

Three basic forest types occur in the Dalton region. The first is the bottom land spruce-hardwood forest. Bottom land spruce-hardwood forests dominate permafrost-free zones and are very productive in the taiga. These forests are usually found along active rivers and streams, where the thawing action of moving water creates a thin unfrozen band along the banks. When rivers pass through the hills, these forests may reach only a few hundred yards on either side of the river. Where the surrounding area is flat, they may reach for several miles.

Bottom land spruce-hardwood forests begin with willow and alder, along with such shrubs as horsetail and dwarf fireweed. Willows are popular with moose. This is partly why moose are so often seen along riverbanks. Over time, willow and alder are replaced by balsam poplar and black cottonwood, and eventually with white spruce. When spruce trees take over, after about 100 years, these forests develop a thick understory of feathermosses and a layer of such shrubs and wildflowers as lingonberry, rose, high bush cranberry, twinflower, and horsetail. This thick understory ties up soil nutrients and cools temperatures underground. Eventually—after approximately 300 years—black spruce replaces the white spruce.

The second forest type found in the Dalton region is the lowland spruce-hardwood forest. Lowland spruce-hardwood forests are found along the terraces above river bottoms. These forests sit where permafrost is close to the surface, sometimes within fifteen to twenty inches. Lowland spruce-hardwood forests are easily recognized by the crooked, stunted black spruce that are their trademark. These forests often have

Arctophila fluva grows throughout the Arctic Coastal Plain. It lives both on land and in water. Its bright red leaves brighten the landscape in the fall. It is a primary species in revegetating the landscape.

an understory of bog moss, dwarf birch, Labrador tea, blueberry, lingonberry, crowberry, cloudberry, and bog cranberry.

The third forest type is the upland spruce-hardwood forest. Upland spruce-hardwood forests are the most common of all forests in the region. Black spruce is the dominant tree of this forest, although white spruce, paper birch, and quaking aspen are also common, particularly on south-facing slopes. Upland spruce-hardwood forests extend to treeline at the arctic tundra on the Chandalar Shelf (Mile 235.3). These forests also extend to treeline on the alpine tundra near Finger Mountain (Mile 95). Upland spruce-hardwood forest floors are usually covered with feathermosses and lichens, along with Labrador tea, blueberry, resin birch, and diamondleaf willow.

Tundra

Tundra along the highway comes in two varieties: alpine tundra and arctic tundra. Dry, barren alpine tundra occurs south of the Brooks Range on peaks above 2,500 feet, the point where trees no longer grow. Above this point is a thin band of high shrubs, followed by alpine tundra. Alpine tundra is comprised mainly of lichens, white mountain avens, moss campion, and saxifrage. Lapland rosebay, lingonberry, bearberry, bistort, and bellflower also grow in alpine tundra. The stretch of highway near Finger Rock (Mile 97.5) provides an excellent example of alpine tundra.

Arctic tundra, divided into moist and wet categories, is known for the splendor of its wildflowers. Moist tundra is the dominant plant community north of Atigun Pass (Mile 246.8). It ranges from areas of water-saturated soils covered entirely by cottongrass to densely vegetated stands of dwarf shrubs. Several shrubs and wildflowers contribute to the wide array of moist tundra colors, including bright yellow avens, white cloudberry and bistort, pink lingonberry, and brilliant purple Lapland rosebay.

Wet tundra is common along the small lakes and ponds of the Coastal Plain. Dwarf shrubs grow on low ridges and aquatic plants grow in standing water. Bog cranberry, buttercup, bog rosemary, and cloudberry all thrive in wet tundra.

Shrubs

In addition to contributing to the understory of forest communities, shrubs fill gaps where neither forests nor tundra dominate. High shrub communities of Richardson willow, Sitka alder, mountain alder, Jacob's Ladder, and horsetail occur as a transitional zone between upland spruce-hardwood forests and alpine tundra at the 2,500-foot mark south of the Brooks Range.

Low shrub-muskeg bogs occur in lowland areas where conditions are too wet for tree growth, such as partially filled ponds, low-lying depressions in flood plains, and abandoned stream channels. These bogs can be formed from existing forests by one of three processes: (1) by peat taking over small ponds, (2) by forest land becoming swamped when mosses gather in low areas and hold water, and (3) by the thawing of ice-rich permafrost, which creates a water-filled depression. Low shrub communities range from dense sedges and mosses to shrub thickets of willow and alder.

Wildlife

The Dalton Highway region is home to a diverse collection of wildlife species. Big game animals roam from Livengood to the Arctic Ocean, as do several predators. Fur-bearers also make homes throughout the region. A few birds live full-time in the area, and millions more vacation there each summer. Breakup reveals rivers and lakes filled with fish.

Mammals

Mammals of the Dalton region vary from the mouse-like pika to the giant bull moose. Caribou are the most numerous of the large mammals, with thirteen distinct herds, including the massive 140,000-head Porcupine herd. These large deer can weigh as much as 700 lbs., although most bulls weigh between 350 and 400 lbs. Cows average 175-225 lbs. Caribou are the only member of the deer family in which both sexes grow antlers.

Caribou are migratory animals, often traveling more than 2,700 miles annually, the greatest trek of any large land animal. Caribou in the Central Arctic Herd—the most commonly seen in the Dalton region—spend the summer on the Arctic Coastal Plain. They often can be seen finding shade under sections of elevated pipeline. After the mating season in September and October, the Central Arctic Herd migrates south across the Brooks Range to spend the winter in the Interior. Each spring, the herd moves back across the Brooks Range to calving areas along the northeast corner of Alaska and the North Yukon National

Caribou are the most commonly seen large mammal in Alaska's northern regions. They are frequently seen in Prudhoe Bay and the other oil fields in the area. These four bulls rest along one of the feeder pipelines that brings oil to the trans-Alaska pipeline.

Park in Canada. They then move back to the North Slope for the summer.

The moose is another prominent member of the deer family. It is also the largest of all Alaska land mammals, weighing up to 1,600 lbs. Long, awkward-looking legs, short bodies, and big noses give moose an almost comedic appearance. Bull moose antlers, which reach full size when the moose is six or seven years of age, are one of the most impressive racks in nature.

Moose survive in a variety of habitats. In low-lying areas, such as the river bottoms, they spend the summer moving among the shallow ponds, eating sedges, willows, and pond weeds. In mountainous regions, they stay near treeline, eating the buds of birch and aspen. Sometimes moose create a browse line six to eight feet above the ground where they have eaten all the fresh shoots of their favorite trees.

Dall sheep spend their lives in the most rugged, dangerous terrain. Most Dall sheep in the region reside among the high peaks of the Brooks Range. Sometimes a few can be seen at Atigun Pass (Mile 246.8). These high alpine ridges provide excellent escape routes for the sheep, who face predation from golden eagles, wolves, and grizzly bears. Dall sheep usually only descend from their lofty perches when food is scarce during the winter.

The musk ox is a heavy, hairy animal with wide, thick horns. Adult males stand about five feet tall at the shoulder and weigh approximately 600 lbs. Females weigh about 350 lbs. They are permanent residents of the Arctic Coastal Plain. Groups of from fifteen to twenty can occasionally be seen along the North Slope.

The original Alaska musk oxen had all disappeared by 1850, hunted for their extraordinarily warm fur. Those found on the Coastal Plain today are descended from a group that was transplanted there in 1969 and 1970. This group has flourished on the Coastal Plain, partly because they have few effective natural predators. When attacked, musk oxen encircle their young and face their enemies, using their powerful heads and horns to fight off their attackers.

There is no lack of predators in the Dalton region. Wolves are the most effective and are the primary hunters of caribou, moose, Dall sheep, and musk oxen. Wolves usually travel in packs of from two to twelve animals (although packs can have as many as thirty-six to forty members). They have a highly developed social order ruled by a dominance hierarchy. Packs usually establish a 200-600 square mile home range.

Grizzly, black, and polar bears all inhabit the region. Black bears are the most abundant of the three species and can be found throughout the region south of the Brooks Range. Black bears are also the smallest

Alaska bears, weighing 180-200 lbs. They feed primarily on berries and other vegetation, along with salmon if it is available.

Grizzlies, also known as brown bears (the two are now grouped as one species), and polar bears are closely related. They are similar in size (up to 1,400 lbs.), but have evolved to fit their different habitats. Grizzlies make their homes throughout most of the region, while polar bears live almost exclusively on the frozen Arctic Ocean. While grizzly bears are not significant predators, feeding mostly on berries, vegetation, and roots,—and salmon, of course—polar bears are pure carnivores, feeding on ice-inhabiting ringed seals and bearded seals, and small animals, eggs, and carcasses. Polar bears have also adapted to life on the sea ice by growing a short snout and ears, fur-covered feet, and a water-repellent white coat with thick underfur.

There is an abundance of smaller mammals in the highway region. Fur-bearers, including the arctic and red fox, the land otter, the marten, the mink, and the snowshoe hare, make their homes in the region. Beavers build dams on several streams near the highway. Coyotes, relative newcomers to Alaska, hunt snowshoe hares, marmots, and ground squirrels as far north as the Brooks Range. The lynx, the only cat native to Alaska, hunts snowshoe hare and other small mammals. Wolverines, whose fur is commonly used for parka trim and hoods, hunt everything from snowshoe hare to caribou and young moose. Mouse-like lemmings are a staple food for such predators as arctic foxes, wolves, wolverines, and snowy owls.

A few mammals are found in the waters off the Arctic Coast. The "belukha," or white whale, migrates through the Arctic Ocean between Canada and Southeast Alaska winter grounds. Both the ringed seal and bearded seal, called "ugruk" by Alaska Natives, inhabit the waters off the northern coast, and are staples for polar bears in the area.

Birds

Nearly 400 bird species make their homes in the Dalton region. These species can be divided into two groups: resident species, which stay in the region year-round, and migratory species, which spend the summer months in the region but migrate as far away as South America, Africa, and Antarctica in the fall. There is no room here for a comprehensive list of these species, but a few birds merit special note.

Perhaps the most culturally significant of all resident bird species along the Dalton route is the raven. Ravens play an important role in many Native Alaskan creation myths, and raven symbolism can still be found in the art, music, and dance of many Native peoples. Ravens are the largest all-black birds in the world. They are deceptively fast flyers, can make over thirty separate vocal sounds, and have very long lives—often in excess of thirty years. They can be seen south of the Brooks Range, usually at trash barrels and other waste disposal sites along the Dalton. Ravens are notorious scavengers.

The willow ptarmigan, the Alaska state bird, lives above treeline throughout the region. Willow ptarmigans resemble small grouse, except that they have white wings and their plumage turns completely white during the winter. They regularly migrate as they search for food during the winter. Willow ptarmigan young can fly when they are nine to ten days old.

Several birds of prey reside year-round in the area. Northern harriers, or marsh hawks, are the most commonly seen of the birds of prey along the highway. Watch for low-flying raptors with white rumps—not tail feathers, rumps—as you travel the Dalton. Goshawks live in birch and aspen stands south of the Brooks Range, where they hunt grouse, ptarmigan, ducks, and snowshoe hares. Golden eagles make their homes throughout the region, building large, strong nests in tall trees or cliffs. Golden eagles can occasionally be seen at Ice Cut (Mile 324.9). Gyrfalcons, the largest of the falcons, also nest in cliffs from the Interior to the North Slope. Bald eagles can sometimes be seen along the Yukon River.

Migratory geese species, including Canada geese, emperor's geese, white-fronted geese, black brants, and lesser snow geese, are the most numerous of all the birds in Alaska, numbering in the hundreds of thousands. All of these species except the lesser snow geese spend their summers along the Yukon River wetlands; snow geese summer on the Arctic Coastal Plain. The Yukon Flats Wildlife Refuge and the Kanuti

Wildlife Refuge are both prime habitat for these summer visitors.

Several duck species, including eiders, harlequins, mallards, pintails, gadwalls, northern shovelers, scoters, and mergansers, migrate to the area each summer. Ducks are physically similar to but smaller than geese, and spend more time in the water. Like geese, ducks migrate from southern winter grounds ranging from Alaska's Aleutian Chain to South America. The majority of these ducks summer in the Yukon River basin and the wildlife refuges, although several species move to the Arctic Coastal Plain after breakup.

A number of other migratory birds may be seen along the Dalton route. Crane-like greater and lesser yellowlegs spend their summer on the shores of shallow ponds and lakes. Groups of plovers and sandpipers can often be seen at larger bodies of water. Long-tailed yeagers are very common in June and July. Phalaropes, tame enough to be approached by humans, come to Alaska from South America and Africa. Northern wheatears arrive from winter grounds in South Africa. Terns, members of the gull family, arrive after 25,000-mile flights from Antarctica. Sandhill cranes and trumpeter, tundra, and whooping swans all summer along the Yukon River. The peregrine falcon, or duck hawk, is a migratory bird of prey that summers in the Dalton region. Fifty-one species of sparrows migrate to Alaska each year.

Fish

Both fresh-water and "anadromous"—salt-water fish that return to fresh water to spawn—fish species inhabit the streams and lakes of the region. Most of these species are open to sport fishing.

Chum, coho, and king, or chinook, salmon pass through many of the region's rivers and streams as they head to spawning grounds. These salmon spawn near the headwaters of the Yukon River, traveling up to 2,000 miles from the ocean, farther than any other salmon in the world. Note that it is illegal to keep salmon caught throughout most of the Dalton region.

Arctic grayling are the most well-known sport fish in the region.

They inhabit nearly all flowing waters in the area and have been introduced into many lakes south of the Brooks Range. Arctic grayling are very willing to take bait, which has made them extremely popular with anglers.

Whitefish are the most abundant fish species in the region. One or more members of the whitefish family—which includes round whitefish; broad and humpback whitefish; bering, arctic, and least cisco; and sheefish—can be found in almost every freshwater habitat in the region. Burbot—the only true freshwater cod—can be recognized by dorsal and anal fins that extend from mid-body almost to their tails, and are found from the Yukon River to the Brooks Range. The blackfish, which can live off atmospheric oxygen, is found throughout the Interior. Arctic char and Dolly Varden inhabit streams and lakes north of Coldfoot (Mile 175). Lake trout can be found in several lakes between Pump Station No. 4 (Mile 269.2) and the Toolik Construction Camp (Mile 284.2). The duck-billed northern pike lives in waters from the Interior to the Arctic Coastal Plain.

Recreation

To simply drive the Dalton Highway is to get but a small taste of what the region has to offer. As you travel the highway, you can choose from a wide range of recreational activities that allow you to better feel this wild land. From gold-panning to river-rafting, fishing to backpacking to sightseeing, there are many options available to anyone who wants the full Dalton Highway experience.

Camping

Camping is allowed throughout the Dalton Highway region except for within two road miles of the South Fork Koyukuk River bridge (Mile 156.1), within one mile upstream or downstream of the bridge, and in the vicinity of the University of Alaska research station at Toolik Lake (Mile 284.2). Campsites are provided at Hess Creek (Mile 23.8), the Yukon River (Mile 55.5), Five Mile Camp (Mile 60.4), the Arctic Circle (Mile 115.3), Prospect Creek/Jim River (Mile 135.7), Coldfoot (Mile 175), and Marion Creek (Mile 179.9). All of these sites are undeveloped.

The fun of camping in the Dalton region is that you do not have to use an established campsite. Millions of acres of back country are available, and you may pick almost any spot you like. If you just need an overnight stopover along the highway, you may want to use one of the established sites. If you're looking for a true wilderness experience, however, you will want to leave the highway and disappear into the back country. As you do, remember that in the arctic you must be well-prepared and self-sufficient. The region is a true wilderness, and emergency services are not readily available.

If you decide to camp in the wilderness, select your campsite with care. It can be very disquieting to find out in the wee hours of the morning that you've set up camp in the middle of a bear trail. Look for a level, well-drained spot in the open if possible; gravel bars work quite nicely. Gravel bars also have fewer mosquitoes than other sites, and they allow you to stay off fragile arctic vegetation. As an added plus, next spring's high water will erase any sign of your presence. Be careful, however; water levels can rise onto gravel bars quickly. Do not camp on a gravel bar if it has been raining heavily or if the weather has been especially warm, which increases glacial runoff.

If you are unable to camp on a gravel bar, look for a spot with strong vegetation, such as moss or heath, rather than more fragile lichens. Move camp every two to three days to minimize damage to the area. By law you cannot camp in the same location along the Dalton longer than fourteen days in any twenty-eight-day period.

When setting up your campsite, be sure to locate your toilet facilities at least 150 feet away from streams, rivers, and lakes. Wash dishes and bathe at least 100 feet away from these water sources. Use biodegradable soaps. Boil or chemically purify all drinking water. *Giardiasis*, a waterborne intestinal disease, is common in Alaska. If possible, use a gas or alcohol stove for cooking. Do not bury your litter—collect it and pack it out.

If you plan to camp in the back country, leave a travel plan describing your trip with friends, and notify them when you return. Practice minimum impact camping. Your goal should be that when you break camp, you have left no trace you were ever there.

Backpacking

Thousands of backpackers experience the Dalton region's beauty and wildness each summer. Backpacking is one of the most popular activities in the region. This is a backpacker's paradise, with terrain ranging from flat plains and lowlands to steep mountainsides and tundra-covered peaks.

There are no officially established trails in the Dalton area, although several locations along the route are popular with hikers. These locations include the areas around Bonanza Creek (Mile 124.7), the Bettles/Dietrich River (Mile 207), Galbraith Lake (Mile 274.8), and anywhere through the Brooks Range. Due to poor drainage of lowland soils—often making for wet, swampy conditions—hiking is most enjoyable on uplands and higher ridges. If you plan to backpack, you are free to set out wherever you want, following your own desires and abilities. There are no public cabins in the region.

If you plan to hike, observe safe backpacking practices. Know your abilities and do not exceed them. If you plan to hike in the Brooks Range, do not attempt glacier crossings unless you have mountaineering equipment and experience. Be aware of the temperature, especially above treeline where you are not protected from the wind. Hypothermia is a constant danger. Know how to recognize and treat it. Contact your local American Red Cross for hypothermia information. Be especially aware of wildlife. You are likely to run into some.

Know the area where you are planning to hike. Carry a compass and appropriate topographical maps and know how to use them. Use a 1:36,360 (1 inch = 1 mile) map; a 1:250,000 map doesn't provide enough detail. Don't forget mosquito repellent. The visitor center in Coldfoot has information on hiking throughout the highway region. You can find the correct topographical map at the U.S. Geological Survey (USGS). (See *Index of Agencies.*)

Be considerate of others and of nature as you travel the back country. The Dalton region is interspersed with privately owned land. Please don't disturb these areas. Cabins and food caches that seem to be abandoned usually aren't. The owner needs whatever is stored there. Also, if you see a trail forming in the back country, please choose an alternate route. Plants in this region take years to recover from overuse.

As with any trip into the back country, leave a travel plan describing your hike with friends, and notify them when you return. And remember to practice minimum impact hiking—leave no trace you were ever there.

Recreational Gold-panning

Much of the Dalton area was developed as a direct result of gold-mining, and several productive mines still operate in the area. Recreational gold-mining using metal detectors, gold pans, rocker boxes, and sluices is allowed without a permit in most of the Dalton Highway region.

If you would like to pan for gold along the highway, remember three things:

- First, you may not pan for gold in the pipeline right-of-way.

- Second, you must be certain that the area is not already claimed.

- Third, you should consider the environmental impact of gold-panning when choosing a site.

The BLM has the most accurate information on current mining claims in the region. Call them and check on the area you hope to pan before heading up the highway. (See *Index of Agencies.*)

Pan for gold only in active stream beds or on unvegetated gravel bars. Do not pan on vegetated riverbanks, where you could harm plant life. Wash soil along the edges of streams, not directly into the stream flow. The silt and decaying organic matter in the soil could cut off the oxygen supply to fish eggs buried in spawning beds.

Boating

There are a number of waterways in the Dalton Highway region that can be floated by canoes, kayaks, and rafts. There are also several such areas in the Kanuti and Yukon Flats National Wildlife Refuges. Due to the lack of roads, however, relatively few waterways allow you to both put in and take out at a spot accessible by automobile. You can charter an airplane to fly you to an otherwise inaccessible river, but this is very expensive. Because the options are so limited, a river trip in the region requires careful planning. Never put in without knowing for certain just when and where you are going to take out and how you are going to get back. Always drive to both your put-in and take-out spots before starting a river trip to make sure both are accessible. Summer thaws turn many trails along the Dalton into impassable quagmires.

The same spot you used earlier in the season may not be accessible anymore. Without careful planning, you could find yourself up the creek without a paddle, so to speak.

You can plan a river trip in the region on waters ranging from Class I to Class IV on the International Scale of River Difficulty. For example, a float trip on the Middle Fork Koyukuk from near Sukakpak Mountain (Mile 204.3) to Coldfoot (Mile 175) is a slow, two-day, Class I trip. A trip down the Sagavanirktok from Mile 336 to Prudhoe Bay is an eight-day, Class IV adventure for highly experienced boaters in covered canoes and kayaks.

Alaska rivers pose special dangers to boaters. Water levels can change rapidly, especially in glacially fed rivers. Warm days cause heavy glacial melt, raising river levels drastically. Heavy summer rains can bring rivers to flood stage in a few hours. Conversely, long dry spells may mean many shallow areas.

Hypothermia is a constant danger for boaters in the Dalton Highway region. Northern river water is very cold, often between 35° and 45° Fahrenheit. If you capsize, you have only a few minutes before the cold water immobilizes you. Sweepers and log jams are common in these rivers, and can quickly tip a canoe or raft. You must be constantly on the alert for danger. If you have any doubts about a stretch of river, stop, scout ahead, and line down from the bank or portage around.

Wear an approved life jacket at all times. Take a compass and applicable topographical maps. Maps are available from the U.S. Geological Survey office. Know your paddling skills—don't expect to learn them on the river. Before attempting a boating trip in the Dalton Highway region, you should be a proficient boater.

Take safety items with you, including at least one complete change of clothes, waterproof matches, a 50- or 100-foot throw rope for rescues, extra paddles, a first aid kit, emergency flares, boat repair materials, insect repellent, sunscreen, and dark glasses. Securely tie all gear into your boat.

Always leave a float plan describing your trip with friends, and notify them when you return. For more detailed information on boating safety, equipment, and river routes, contact the BLM. (See *Index of Agencies*.)

Sightseeing

The Dalton Highway region is so densely packed with things to see that sightseeing is not an occasional activity; it is what you will be doing the entire time you are on the highway.

Certain locations are especially popular as sightseeing spots. These include Finger Mountain (Mile 97.5), Cathedral Lake (Mile 165), Sukakpak Mountain (Mile 203.5), Chandalar Shelf (Mile 237.1), Atigun Pass (Mile 246.8), and the Sagwon Bluffs (Mile 350). This list contains only a small number of the many beautiful sights. The *Travel Log* lists particularly good viewpoints and areas.

To fully enjoy the sights, bring a camera. Binoculars are nice, too. Remember to stop only in pullouts or areas where you can pull your vehicle completely off the highway.

Wildlife Watching

Wildlife watching is extremely popular with Dalton Highway visitors. Nothing is quite as spectacular as watching a herd of caribou move majestically across a ridge line or seeing a moose and her calf forage peacefully among a clump of willows. While there is no guarantee that you will see a particular animal at any specific location, you can increase your chances by knowing where and when to look.

As a general guideline, watch for moose, bears, and smaller mammals feeding in low-lying areas with lots of shrubs and saplings. Moose also feed in marshy areas —ponds, creeks, and river bottoms. Several species of waterfowl also congregate in these same marshy areas. Watch for black bears around open stands of aspen growing on the sandy domes between the Yukon River and Coldfoot.

Watch for Dall sheep in the rocky, open alpine tundra of the Brooks Range—especially at Atigun Pass. Caribou are widespread in the region. Watch for them everywhere, especially high above timberline, where they go to avoid insects. Bears also move to the tundra later in the fall. Arctic foxes and musk oxen can sometimes be seen on the North Slope. Most wild animals move around more at dawn and dusk, so be on alert at these times.

Even though the animals you see appear calm and friendly, they can still be quite dangerous. The Alaska Department of Fish and Game suggests the following rules while watching wild animals:

- Keep your distance. Most wild animals react with alarm when approached by humans, and can act unpredictably. You are too close to an animal if:
  - The animal displays aggressive or nervous behavior;
  - It begins moving away from you;
  - The hairs on its neck and shoulders stand erect;
  - It raises its head high, ears pointed towards you; or
  - It lowers its head, ears back, to charge.

- Use proper equipment. Quality binoculars or a spotting scope let you observe from a safe distance. A telephoto lens and a tripod allow you to get close-up photos without putting yourself in danger.

- Blend in. Wear muted colors and sit quietly—unless there is the possibility of bears nearby.

- Always give animals the right-of-way on game trails.

- Avoid meeting or getting between a bear and her cubs or a moose and her calves.

- Don't hurry. The more time you remain in an area, the greater your chances of spotting wildlife.

The best way to gain information on wildlife habitat and behavior is to purchase a good field guide. Several are listed in *Suggested Reading*.

Hunting

Hunting with firearms is prohibited within the boundaries of a hunting and fishing corridor that stretches for five miles on either side of the Dalton Highway. This corridor stretches from the Yukon River crossing (Mile 55.5) to a point about three miles south of the Deadhorse Airport (Mile 411.1). North of this point no hunting is allowed. The corridor passes through five different game management units, each with its own seasons, bag limits, and restrictions. Bow hunting is allowed within the corridor. All bow hunters must possess an International Bow hunters Education Program (IBEP) card. Hunting with firearms is allowed outside the corridor. But take note: It's no easy task to haul a caribou or moose the five miles from outside the corridor back to the road.

Big game species open to bow hunting include black and grizzly bear, caribou, moose, musk ox, sheep, wolf, and wolverine. Small game, such as grouse, hare, ptarmigan, and most waterfowl may also be taken. Fur-bearers open to hunting include arctic fox, red fox, coyote, lynx, and red squirrel. Most seasons start in July, August, or September and continue until the following spring or early summer, although some animals may be hunted year-round.

Before planning a hunt in the Dalton Highway area, get a current copy of the hunting rules, regulations, and fees from the Alaska Department of Fish and Game. The department also has handouts which specifically discuss hunting in the Dalton Highway region. Licenses, tags, and state duck stamps are available from any license vendor or by mail from the Alaska Department of Fish and Game, Licensing Section. (See *Index of Agencies.*) Federal duck stamps are available at U.S. post offices.

Fishing

Sport fishing is allowed along the entire length of the highway, and several fish species are found in the region's waterways. Most sport fishing occurs within the ten-mile hunting and fishing corridor. All fish except salmon may legally be taken within this corridor. Arctic grayling is the most abundant fish, although Dolly Varden, lake trout, burbot, and record-class northern pike are also taken. Many species of whitefish, including round whitefish, least cisco, bering cisco, arctic cisco, broad whitefish, humpback whitefish, and sheefish, inhabit the region's rivers and streams. However, these are not normally taken as sport fish.

The best time to fish along the Dalton Highway is from July to mid-September. Many of the rivers and streams are high and muddy during most of June as the snow melts in the Brooks Range. As a general rule, the fishing improves the farther you get from the highway. Streams, rivers, and lakes next to the road have been heavily fished for several years. Since fish grow and reproduce very slowly this far north, populations in these areas tend to remain low. Your best fishing will be in areas rarely visited, where populations haven't been heavily affected. The Alaska Department of Fish and Game encourages anglers to practice catch and release techniques using barbless hooks to maintain fish populations.

Most anglers are required to purchase a sport fishing license. Bag limits vary with species and location. In addition, the Department of Fish and Game may, at any time, close specific bodies of water or the entire area to sport fishing if it feels that stock is being depleted. Before fishing in the Dalton region, obtain a copy of current rules and regulations from the Department of Fish and Game.

Guides and Outfitters

Dozens of guides and outfitters are registered in the state to take people on hunting and fishing trips and river-running excursions. The entire list of guides cannot fit here, but you can obtain a copy by contacting the Department of Commerce and Economic Development, Division of Occupational Licensing. (See *Index of Agencies.*)

Wildlife Refuges and National Parks

National wildlife refuges and national parks are set aside to preserve wild habitat for the animals that live within them. Three refuges and one park have been established near the Dalton Highway. Although outside the Dalton Highway region as defined in this guide, they are included because the highway region is the jumping off point to these lands for many visitors. Visitors to these public lands will find a wealth of opportunities. You are free to hike, camp, hunt, fish, boat, or just enjoy the scenery.

Yukon Flats National Wildlife Refuge

The Yukon Flats National Wildlife Refuge lies east of the highway from the Yukon River Crossing (Mile 55.5) to approximately Disaster Creek (Mile 210.5). This 8.63 million-acre wildlife refuge is formed by a vast wetland basin known as the Yukon Flats. The Yukon River runs 300 miles through the refuge, which also contains more than 40,000 shallow lakes and innumerable ponds and sloughs.

Obviously, water is the dominant feature of the Yukon Flats National Wildlife Refuge. Millions of migrating birds, including mallards, shovelers, Canada and white-fronted geese, loons, grebes, and sandhill cranes, converge on the Yukon Flats each May. More than 50,000 canvasbacks nest in the refuge. Moose, caribou, and black and grizzly bear also make their homes in the Yukon Flats.

Most recreational activities in the refuge are related to motorized and non-motorized boating. Before planning a trip to the Yukon Flats Wildlife Refuge, contact the refuge manager. (See *Index of Agencies.*)

Kanuti National Wildlife Refuge

The Kanuti National Wildlife Refuge lies west of the highway. The refuge is twenty-five miles away at its southern border near No Name Creek (Mile 79.1), but within seven miles of the corridor at the Arctic Circle (Mile 115.3). This 1.6 million-acre refuge lies in a wetland basin formed by the Kanuti and Koyukuk rivers. These two rivers, which form the heart of the Kanuti National Wildlife Refuge, unite near the western boundary of the refuge before joining the Yukon.

Like the Yukon Flats, the Kanuti National Wildlife Refuge is dominated by water. Therefore, most recreational activities in Kanuti involve boating. More than 100 different bird species, including swans, ducks, loons, and cranes, have been observed on the refuge. Peregrine falcons and other raptors hunt and breed from the rocky cliffs of the Kanuti River Canyon on the western border of the refuge. The refuge supports several species of fish, as well as moose, caribou, wolves, and black and grizzly bears. Before making a trip to the Kanuti National Wildlife Refuge, contact the refuge manager. (See *Index of Agencies*.)

Arctic National Wildlife Refuge

The Arctic National Wildlife Refuge, or ANWR, lies east of the Dalton Highway from about Coldfoot (Mile 175) to Galbraith Lake (Mile 274.8). ANWR comes closest to the highway near Atigun Pass, at the Continental Divide. This nearly 20 million-acre refuge spans the Brooks Range and is the northernmost unit in the National Wildlife Refuge System. The most numerous residents of ANWR are the 140,000 caribou of the Porcupine herd. Moose, Dall sheep, and grizzly bear also inhabit the refuge.

Most ANWR visitors arrange charter air service from Fairbanks to the refuge. Once within the refuge, visitors are on their own. There are no trails within ANWR, so you can hike and camp wherever you wish. For more information on ANWR, contact the refuge manager. (See *Index of Agencies*.)

Gates of the Arctic National Park and Preserve

This 8.4 million-acre park and preserve sits to the west of the Dalton Highway from near the South Fork Koyukuk River Crossing (Mile 156.1) to near Galbraith Lake (Mile 274.7). Gates of the Arctic got its name from Robert Marshall, a frequent traveler in the region from 1929 to 1939 (see *History*). Marshall viewed two peaks within the park—Frigid Crags and Boreal Mountain—as the gateway from Alaska's central Brooks Range into the arctic regions of the Far North; thus, Gates of the Arctic National Park.

Gates of the Arctic encompasses a wide variety of landforms, from the foothills of Alaska's Interior to the ragged-peaked Brooks Range to the rolling hills of the Arctic Coastal Plain. The park contains major portions of the range and habitat of the 400,000-animal Western Arctic caribou herd, the largest caribou herd in the world. Grizzly and black bear, wolf, moose, and Dall sheep are also found in the park.

Gates of the Arctic National Park and Preserve is maintained as a remote, unpopulated wilderness, with no trails or visitor services. Although hunting is allowed in the three wildlife refuges just mentioned, it is prohibited in all but the preserve section of Gates of the Arctic National Park and Preserve. Before making a trip to Gates of the Arctic, contact the park superintendent. (See *Index of Agencies*.)

Bear Encounters

Nearly any recreational activity in the Dalton Highway region could bring you in contact with bears. This can be a frightening experience. If you are prepared and know what to do, however, a bear encounter could turn out to be the crowning event of your Dalton Highway experience. Whatever recreational activities you plan, it is important that you know proper bear encounter guidelines. *Bear Facts*, a pamphlet published in cooperation with several government agencies, suggests:

When you enter bear territory (most of the region):

■ Beware of your surroundings. Look for bear.

■ Make your presence known. Whistle, hum a tune, talk to your companions. Bears will generally avoid you if they can.

■ Avoid game trails if possible, especially if they lead through tall brush, and never follow bear tracks.

■ Avoid areas where you see or smell fish or animal carcasses, or where you see fresh bear droppings.

If you camp:

■ Camp away from game trails.

■ Keep a clean camp.

■ Cook and eat away from your tent.

■ Avoid smelly foods like bacon and smoked fish.

■ Keep food smells off your clothing.

■ Store all food away from your campsite.

■ Hang food out of reach of bears, or store it in airtight or specially designed bear-proof containers.

If you come face-to-face with a bear:

- Do not panic.

- Identify yourself: talk calmly, wave your arms. Back away slowly, but if the bear follows, STOP. DO NOT RUN. Bears have been clocked at speeds of up to thirty-five miles per hour. Continue making noise—DO NOT make bear noises or high-pitched squeals—and waving your arms.

- If a grizzly bear comes in contact with you, fall to the ground and play dead. Lie flat on your stomach or curl into a ball with your hands behind your head.

- If a black bear attacks you, fight back as hard as you can.

Traveling the Dalton Highway

The Dalton Highway region, although beautiful and inviting, can be a dangerous place. To safely enjoy the trip, you should enter it fully prepared for the challenges you may face. The following are tips, suggestions, and ideas to keep in mind as you plan your trip. Make your preparations carefully so that you can thoroughly enjoy the adventure that lies ahead.

When to Go

Although the Dalton Highway is open year-round, almost all visitors travel between mid-May and the first of September. During this time, the area is relatively warm and free of snow. Tourist travel during any other time of the year is not advisable. Poor weather makes driving dangerous. After the first of September, most visitors are hunters. Before you begin your Dalton Highway adventure, call the Alaska Department of Transportation's road condition recording at (907) 456-7623.

What to Take

Few services are available along the highway. Consequently, you should be as self-sufficient as possible. As you pack, pick and choose those things from the following lists that meet your plans and goals. Both Anchorage and Fairbanks are modern communities and have additional items you may need.

Clothing

Keep two concepts in mind: comfort and utility. You will be spending a lot of hours driving, and your clothing should allow you to do this comfortably. Your clothing should also reflect the wide range of weather conditions that you may encounter. It may be warm and sunny, with temperatures in the nineties, or it could be cold and wet, with temperatures in the forties or fifties. Bring clothing for both extremes, including a warm coat, rubber boots, and gloves, as well as light shirts, sneakers, and casual slacks or jeans. If you plan recreational activities, bring clothing suitable for those activities—hiking boots, wool socks, brimmed hat, etc.

Recreational Equipment

Don't forget to bring the recreational equipment you will need to match your plans—camping and backpacking gear, gold-panning implements, boating equipment, and fishing tackle. Binoculars, a camera, and several rolls of film are a must.

Miscellaneous

Bring enough food and water to sustain you; there are 239 miles between Coldfoot and Deadhorse. Insect repellent is a must. Alaskans claim that the mosquitoes here haul off children and small animals. Window coverings, sunscreen, and dark glasses are necessities to combat the twenty-four-hour summer sun. Also, make sure you have sufficient cash. Rooms along the highway can cost in excess of $100 per night. Wrecker and repair services cost more than $85 per hour.

Services, Accommodations, and Tours

The only services and accommodations along the Dalton are found at the Yukon River crossing (Mile 56), Coldfoot (Mile 175), and Deadhorse (Mile 414.9). As more and more people drive the highway each year, accommodations fill quickly. If you need lodging during your trip, make reservations well in advance. Don't get stuck sleeping in your car.

If you are driving to Prudhoe Bay and want to tour the oil fields, you must make advance arrangements. To do this, contact one of the following agencies in Deadhorse: North Star Inn, Prudhoe Bay Hotel, or Arctic Caribou Inn.

Below is a list of accommodations and services along the Dalton:

- **Yukon Ventures** has a gas station, garage, restaurant, and rooms. They accept cash, U.S. checks, VISA, and MasterCard. Contact Yukon Ventures at (907) 655-9001.

- **Coldfoot Services** has a gas station, wrecker service, restaurant, phone, and rooms. They accept cash, in-state checks, VISA, MasterCard, American Express, and Discover. Contact Coldfoot Services at (907) 678-9301.

- **Natchiq, Inc.** has wrecker service, garage, equipment rental, and a phone. Contact Natchiq, Inc. at (907) 659-2604.

- **North Star Inn** has a gas station, rooms (with or without meals), showers, TV rental, phone rental, laundry, and Prudhoe Bay tours. Other services include Budget Rent-A-Car, a Ford Authorized Service Center, temporary offices, pad and warehouse space, and equipment rental. They accept cash, checks, VISA, MasterCard, American Express, Discover, and Diners Club. Contact North Star Inn at (907) 659-3160.

- **Prudhoe Bay Hotel** has rooms (with or without meals) and Prudhoe Bay tours. Contact the Prudhoe Bay Hotel at (907) 659-2449.

- **Arctic Caribou Inn** has a gas station, rooms, dinner and breakfast service, showers, and Prudhoe Bay tours. They accept cash, in-state checks, and all major credit cards. Contact the Arctic Caribou Inn at (907) 659-2368.

- **Prudhoe Bay Commercial Center** has a gas station (open twenty-four hours), tire service, Goodyear tire sales, parts (oil, belts, hoses, batteries, AC Delco parts, GM parts, Motorcraft parts, Champion accessories, Ford products), and tools and hardware. Contact the Prudhoe Bay Commercial Center at (907) 659-2400.

Auto Preparation

Preparing your vehicle for this 800-mile (round trip) journey should be a top priority. Nothing can kill the fun of a trip more quickly than a breakdown. Make sure your vehicle can handle the trip, and make sure you have the necessary emergency equipment if it doesn't.

Before starting out, make sure your car is in good shape. Check all belts, hoses, and fluid levels. Is your battery at full strength? Do your windshield wipers work? Have you changed your spark plugs recently? Consider getting a tune-up. Also, be sure your tires are in top shape and are properly inflated. Keeping your tires at the low end of proper inflation helps on this gravel road. Flat tires are one of the most common problems for Dalton Highway travelers.

You may want to install protective covers over your headlights. Flying rocks are a hazard on the highway, and headlight protectors are fairly cheap. The odds are pretty good that your windshield will be hit by a rock before you're through. Mud flaps are also a good idea, both to save the rear area of your own vehicle from gravel and to protect those behind you.

Safety Equipment

Even if you've done everything possible to ensure your vehicle's road-worthiness, you could still have problems. Vehicles seem to have a sadistic sense of timing when it comes to breakdowns. However, there are things you can do to soften the blow if you have car trouble. You should have the following safety items in your car:

- A citizen's band (CB) radio. Most truckers monitor Channel 19 for distress calls;
- Five to ten extra gallons of gasoline;
- Extra automotive fluids;
- A tire jack and lug wrench, tools for changing belts and hoses, a spark plug wrench, and any other tools (pliers, sockets) needed to perform minor repairs on your vehicle;

- One spare headlight, two mounted tires for each size wheel on your vehicle, replacement hoses, electrical wiring and electrician's tape, and spare belts;

- Tire chains if you are traveling early or late in the season;

- A first aid kit;

- Six safety flares and six emergency reflectors;

- Applicable maps;

- A tow chain/rope;

- A shovel;

- A two-day supply of emergency food and drinking water; and

- Spare clothing. Be sure to bring cold-weather clothing, no matter what time of year you travel.

Safe Driving Tips

Observe safe driving practices on the Dalton Highway, for your own safety and the safety of those with whom you share the road. DO NOT exceed the fifty-miles-per-hour speed limit. Always drive with your headlights on and your seat belt fastened. Be especially careful around large trucks. Pull as far as possible to your side of the highway as they approach. Do the same—and slow to a crawl—if one wants to pass. If you park your vehicle, make sure it is completely off the road. Do not block access roads to the pipeline. Be careful if you see a dust cloud headed your way—most likely there is a car or truck inside of it.

Recreational Vehicles

Several extra points should be considered if you take an RV. First, do not exceed your Gross Vehicle Weight Rating. An overloaded motorhome or travel trailer can be very dangerous on this rough gravel highway. It will drastically increase the odds of a tire blowout. Only Yukon Crossing and Coldfoot have dump stations, so make use of them when you can.

Drive no more than forty miles per hour when towing a trailer exceeding eight feet in width. Protect your front trailer windows by installing mud flaps on your car and attaching a protective cover to the front of your trailer. Be especially careful if you run into ice; this can be extremely dangerous with trailers. Ruts, potholes, and other rough road conditions can break axles, hitches, and trailer tongues. Slow down and watch the road carefully. Latch the cupboards and drawers in your RV securely each day. Otherwise, you may find your dinnerware on the floor after a bumpy day's driving.

If You Break Down

If the worst happens and your car becomes disabled, don't panic; if you're prepared you have nothing to fear. First, get your vehicle as far off the road as possible and lay out your reflectors and flares far enough to the front and rear to alert other vehicles before they reach you. Then see if you can find and fix the problem, at least until you can get to the next service center. If you cannot fix it, get on the CB. Nearly 100 trucks travel the highway each day, and most have CBs. You will probably get somebody to answer immediately. Use Channel 19 to give your location (by milepost) and situation. Have them contact help once they get within range of a service center. If you do not have a CB, flag someone down and send them for help. Stay with your vehicle if at all possible. While waiting for help, relax and try to make the most of your situation. Do some exploring. Become an authority on the 100 yards up and down the highway from where you are stuck.

Other Travel Options

Although the majority of Dalton Highway travelers drive their own vehicles, there is more than one way to get up the highway.

Tours

The most popular travel alternative among Dalton travelers is an organized tour. A few companies offer tour packages with regular departures from Fairbanks and Anchorage. Tours save wear and tear on your vehicle, and you can travel with an authority on the area. But don't assume any guide is an authority. Ask how experienced your guide is with the area before signing up with any tour.

If you are traveling with an organized tour group, full accommodations—rooms, meals, etc.—should be arranged for you. Again, don't assume; ask. Find out exactly what is covered in the cost of the tour and what you are expected to add yourself. Groups offering Prudhoe Bay tours should make arrangements with the oil companies to enter the oil fields and take you all the way to the Arctic Ocean. But again, don't assume; ask.

The following organizations provide Dalton Highway tours. For the most current information on tour packages—prices, schedules, availability, and other details—contact the individual organization or your travel agent.

- **Gray Line of Alaska:** 800-544-2206.
- **Northern Alaska Tour Company:** 907-474-8600.
- **Princess Tours:** 800-835-8907.
- **MarkAir/MarkTours:** 800-478-0800 in Alaska; 800-426-6784 outside Alaska. MarkAir/MarkTours offers flight tours to Deadhorse and Prudhoe Bay. You do **not** travel the Dalton Highway itself.

Private Aircraft

Another travel option for the Dalton Highway is flying your private plane along the route. Before taking off, however, contact the Federal Aviation Administration in Anchorage or the Flight Service Center in Fairbanks. (See *Index of Agencies.*) When you call the FAA, ask for the free booklet, *Flight Tips for Pilots in Alaska.* Make sure you get a weather briefing before flying the highway route. Call 800-WX-BRIEF.

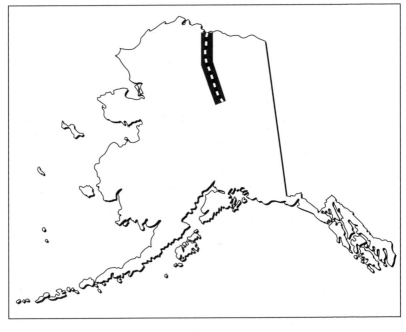

Starting in the heart of Alaska's Interior, the Dalton Highway runs 415 miles to the Arctic Ocean.

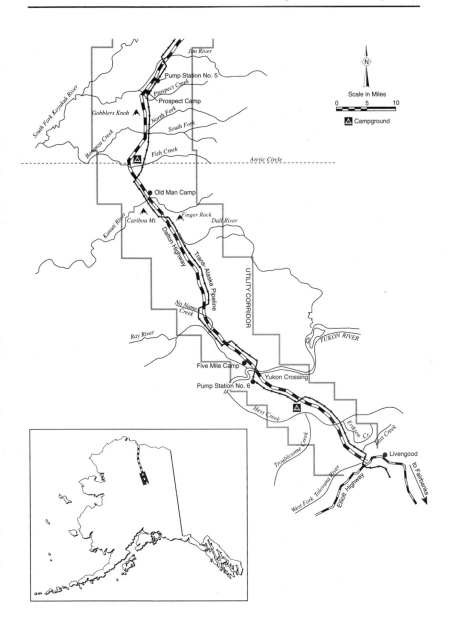

The Dalton Highway from Livengood to Pump Station No. 5

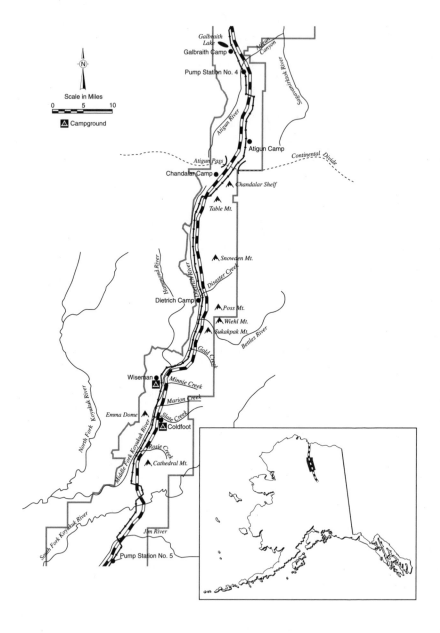

The Dalton Highway from Pump Station No. 5 to Galbraith Lake

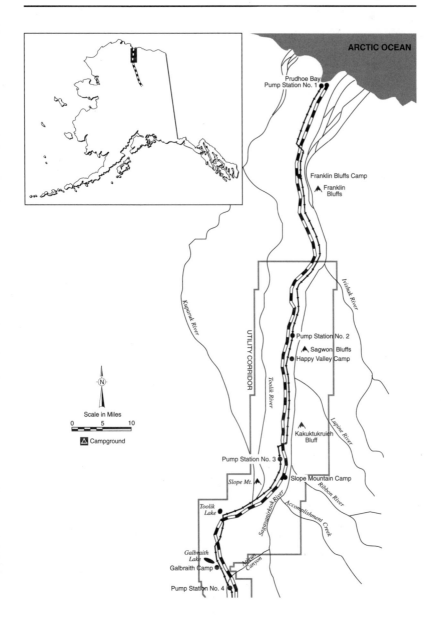

The Dalton Highway from Galbraith Lake to Prudhoe Bay

A Dalton Highway Travel Log

This section gives you mile-by-mile descriptions of the features you will see along the Dalton Highway. It can help keep track of where you are, where you've been, and where you're headed at each point in your trip. Read this section as you plan your trip to find sections or locations that interest you. Follow along as you drive to more fully appreciate what you see. This section should be the most well-used part of the guide by the time you get to Deadhorse.

The Dalton Highway begins somewhat in the middle of nowhere. Livengood is eighty-four miles from Fairbanks, and there is very little but wilderness and road to occupy these miles.

To reach the Dalton Highway from Fairbanks, find the Steese Expressway. The Steese Expressway, named for James G. Steese, an Alaska Road Commission president, covers the first eleven miles between Fairbanks and the Dalton, reaching as far north as the town of Fox. It is paved and kept in pretty good condition year-round. The Steese begins at the intersection of Airport Way and the Richardson Highway at the east side of Fairbanks. Fort Wainwright is to the east and Fairbanks is to the west of this intersection. This is the northern terminus of the Richardson Highway. The Steese takes over at this point as Alaska Route 2.

At Fox, the Steese Expressway becomes the Steese Highway and heads northeast to the town of Circle. The road to the west leads into Fox, which was originally a gold-mining camp. Dalton travelers continue north—straight ahead—at this intersection on what is now the Elliott Highway. The Elliott, named for Malcolm Elliott, an Alaska

73

Road Commission president, covers the seventy-three miles between Fox and Livengood. The first twenty-eight miles of the highway are paved. The remaining forty-five miles to the Dalton are gravel. The Elliott Highway is open year-round and is kept in fairly good shape.

The Steese Expressway and Elliott Highway have several attractions of their own. At Mile 8.4 of the Steese you will find a pipeline viewpoint and display that is very popular with visitors—although, I warn you, you will see plenty of the pipeline over the next 400+ miles. The Fox Spring Picnic Area sits at Mile 0.5 of the Elliott Highway. Picnic tables are provided. The water from Fox Spring is popular with area residents, especially those without indoor plumbing.

The Hilltop Truck Stop and Cafe sits at Elliott Mile 6. This is the last place to get gas before the Yukon River (Mile 56 of the Dalton). The Elliott Highway crosses the Chatanika River and the Lower Chatanika State Recreation Area at Mile 11. Whitefish Campground, on the north side of the Chatanika River, has picnic tables and a picnic shelter, ten campsites, toilets, water, and fishing access. There is also a boat launch area. The campground has wheelchair access. There is a small camping fee.

At Mile 27, the highway passes the White Mountain Summit Trail trail head. The trail is twenty-one miles long and leads to the Borealis-LeFevre cabin, which sits at the banks of the Beaver Creek National Wild River. The cabin can be used for up to three consecutive days for a small fee if you register in advance with the BLM. At Mile 57 the highway passes the Colorado Creek Trail trail head, a nineteen-mile-long trail that also leads to Beaver Creek.

At Elliott Mile 70, the highway passes Livengood Road. The town of Livengood sits about two miles up the road. Three miles following the intersection with Livengood Road, the Elliott Highway turns west to the towns of Manley and Minto, and the Dalton Highway, Alaska Route 11, begins.

Dalton Highway

The Dalton Highway covers the remaining 415 miles from the Elliott Highway to Prudhoe Bay. Read *Traveling the Dalton Highway* and make the proper preparations before attempting to drive this rough gravel road.

There are dozens of pipeline access roads along the route. These are almost always marked with brown signs displaying numbers and letters that tell pipeline workers which access road to use to reach a certain section of the pipeline. Listing these access roads would take most of this travel log, so they will rarely be mentioned. Note that these access roads are for pipeline workers only. Private automobiles are not allowed.

One last note: The odometer on your car may not exactly match the mileposts along the Dalton route. Mine has never matched exactly, and I have been on the highway in several different cars. Don't worry. The log follows the mile signs on the highway, and I've tried to break mileage down to tenths of a mile to be more accurate. As long as you follow this log and watch the highway, you'll know just about where you are. Relax and enjoy.

Mile-by-Mile Log

Mile 0   This is it, the start of the Dalton Highway! From here to the Yukon River (Mile 55.5) is the TAPS Road section of the highway (see *History*).

Mile .2   Travelers ascend a long hill—the first of many. This hill, and the many like it you are about to cross, are typical of Tozitna and Yukon-Tanana terrains. These hills are mainly schist remnants.

Mile 2.9   There is a pulloff to the west.

Mile 5.5   The highway crosses Lost Creek.

Mile 9.3   The pipeline runs parallel to the highway to the northeast.

Mile 12   There is a small pulloff to the west.

Mile 18.9   There is a private road to the west.

Mile 20.9   There is a pulloff to the west.

Mile 23.8   The highway crosses Hess Creek. This creek was named for Mike Hess, the prospector who discovered gold here in 1892. The creek was also called Whymper River, after Western Union Telegraph artist Frederick Whymper, who helped explore the area. Hess Creek is the largest stream between the Dalton/Elliott Highway junction and the Yukon River. There is a pulloff to a gravel bar suitable for parking and camping to the west on the north side of the creek. Arctic grayling are abundant near the Hess Creek bridge, and burbot and northern pike are present farther upstream. If you are a rock hound, this is a good place to get some nice water-polished stones.

Mile 25   There is a pulloff to the west. You can see a pipeline shut-off valve in the valley to the east.

Mile 26.3   There is a pulloff to the east.

Mile 26.5   The pipeline runs close to the highway to the east. This area was burned in a 1967 fire.

Mile 28.4   There is a rock quarry to the west. There are some tight, narrow turns in this section of the highway. Drive carefully!

Mile 36   There is a great view to the west at this point. I've taken some nice pictures here. If you try to get pictures, make sure you pull your vehicle well off the highway.

Mile 38.1   The pipeline passes under the highway.

Mile 38.8   There is a private road to the west.

Mile 41   There is a pulloff to the east.

Mile 43.1   The highway crosses Isom Creek.

Mile 44.6   There is a pulloff to the west.

Mile 47.8   The highway descends towards the Yukon River.

Mile 50.1   There is a pulloff to the east.

Mile 51.2   The road to the east leads to the Yukon River winter ice crossing and hovercraft landing. Before the Yukon River bridge was completed in October 1975, an ice bridge was used during the winter and hovercraft were used during the summer to transport vehicles across the river. The road is now washed out about a mile before reaching the river.

Mile 53.3   The Yukon River can be seen to the north for the first time.

Mile 54   The highway passes the entrance to Pump Station No. 6 to the east. This pump station has a refrigerated foundation that keeps the station from thawing the underlying permafrost. This pump station, along with Stations 8 and 10, has a small refinery that takes crude oil from the pipeline, turns it into fuel, then uses the fuel to operate the engine that drives the pumps, which in turn move the oil down the pipeline. Stations north of the Brooks Range use natural gas for this purpose.

Mile 54.4   An elevated section of the pipeline passes under the highway. There is a pulloff to the west.

Mile 55.5   The highway crosses the Yukon River on the E. L. Patton Bridge. The E. L. Patton Bridge is the only bridge to span the Yukon in Alaska. It is 2,290 feet long and has a six percent grade. E. L. Patton was the president of the pipeline company when the pipeline went into production in 1977. "Yukon" was an Alaska Native word probably meaning "big river." Traders for the Hudson's Bay Co. at Fort Yukon began using the name shortly after establishing the fort in 1847. The Eskimo name for the river is "Kuikpak," which also means "big river." The Yukon River is the largest river in Alaska, the fifth largest in North America, and the twentieth largest in the world. The river heads at Marsh Lake, near the border between Yukon Territory and British Columbia in Canada. It flows over 1,900 miles before it reaches the Bering Sea. Access to the river is via a boat launching ramp to the west on the north side of the river. King and chum salmon, northern pike, arctic grayling, whitefish, and burbot are all present in the Yukon River. Although the muddiness of the water makes for poor recreational line-cast fishing, this is a prime salmon commercial fishing area of the Yukon River. This is a major reason for the existence of Steven's Village, twenty-seven miles upriver of this location. This is the northern terminus of the Tozitna terrain. At this point the landscape changes from the metamorphic schist of the Tozitna to the granitic Ruby terrain. This terrain will dominate from this point to about the town of Coldfoot (Mile 175). For the next hundred miles or so the hills will subside, and such landscape features as tors and sandy domes will become visible.

Mile 55.6   About fifty yards north of the bridge to the east is an excellent camping area. The trail to the area leads under the pipeline, providing an excellent opportunity to look at the pipeline up close and get some great pictures. Being this close to the highway makes things a little noisy, but I've never had a problem getting a decent night's sleep here.

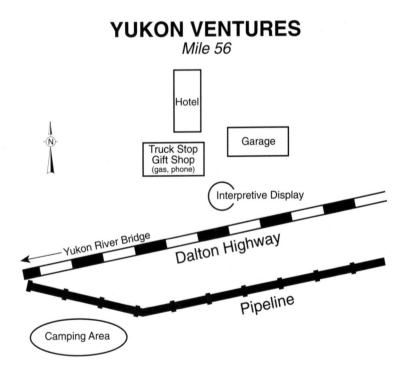

YUKON VENTURES
Mile 56

Mile 56   The highway passes Yukon Ventures. This is the southern border of the BLM-managed lands in the Utility Corridor. Yukon Ventures is operated under BLM permit. Services include food, gas, tire repair, lodging, and telephones. I made use of the tire repair services on one trip, and was in and out in a few minutes. My hunch is they get an awful lot of practice changing tires here. There is also an Alyeska pipeline interpretive display in the parking area, along with a BLM visitor cabin that is staffed in the summer. No services are available between here and Coldfoot (Mile 175, 119 miles north of this point), so if you have any last-minute needs, take care of them here. The area from here to Five Mile Camp (Mile 60.4) is excellent for all kinds of activities, such as camping, boating, hiking, and sightseeing. Watch for black bears in the open aspen stands on several sandy domes from here to the Arctic Circle.

Mile 58.8   The highway passes the entrance to the Alaska Department of Transportation and Public Facilities (DOT/PF) maintenance camp on the west.

Mile 60.4   The highway passes the entrance to Five Mile Camp to the west. Five Mile Camp got its name from its distance from the beginning of the Haul Road at the Yukon River. Few buildings remain at this or the several other camps built along the Dalton route during the highway's construction. There is an undeveloped campground at the camp, and water is available. Treat the water to make sure it is safe to drink.

Mile 60.5   The pipeline passes under the highway. The highway passes close enough to the runway at Five Mile Airport to the east that the highway is closed when a plane takes off or lands. This is another great picture-taking spot. Be prepared to stop if the gate has been lowered.

Mile 61.5   The road to the east leads to the Seven Mile DOT Maintenance Station.

Mile 62   There is a private road to the east.

Mile 65   There is a good view of the pipeline to the west.

Mile 66.8   There is a pulloff to the west.

Mile 69.2   There is a pulloff to the west.

Mile 70.4   The highway passes the Ray River to the west. There are pulloffs to the east and west. These pulloffs can be very muddy when it rains—don't get stuck! The Ray River was named for U.S. Captain Patrick Henry Ray. Captain Ray established a research station in Barrow, Alaska, in 1881 for performing meteorological observations. The Ray River has a number of loops in its course as it passes the highway here. It also contains a number of crescent-shaped lakes, called "oxbows," which are formed when dirt and sand from eroding riverbanks upstream clog the openings of the loops in the river downstream. As the openings of these loops get more and more clogged, they are gradually narrowed until the obstruction becomes too strong for the river current to enter. The river then changes course and the now-isolated loop becomes an oxbow. These oxbows slowly dry up, first changing from a lake to a marsh, then drying completely. The Ray River is popular with anglers. You can reach the river after a short walk, and arctic grayling, northern pike, burbot, and whitefish are all present. The Ray River area is also excellent for float boating and hiking. Watch for moose in the oxbows.

Mile 72.5   The highway crosses Fort Hamlin Hills Creek. The pipeline is visible to the east. There is a pulloff to the west on the north side of the creek. Grayling are abundant in this creek. Fort Hamlin was a trading post of the Alaska Commercial Company. It was located on the Yukon River a few miles east of the Dalton Highway route. The fort was named for Charles Sumner Hamlin, Assistant U.S. Secretary of the Treasury from 1893 to 1897. The Fort Hamlin Hills extend approximately thirty miles to the northwest of Fort Hamlin, to the east of the Dalton.

Mile 73   The highway ascends Sand Hill, so called because geologically it is considered a granitic sandy dome (see *Terrain*). This is the first of several such granitic landscape features of this terrain. The crest of this hill is an excellent spot to look over the scenery—and another great picture-taking spot.

Mile 79.1   The highway crosses No Name Creek—so named by early prospectors—also known as the North Fork of the Ray River. Fishing for arctic grayling is good here in May and June, although water levels drop by midsummer, making the creek a poor fishing spot. There is a pulloff to the east on the south side of the creek.

Mile 82   An unnamed peak, unofficially called "Castle Mountain" because of its appearance, can be seen to the east.

Mile 86   The large valley you can see to the east is part of the Yukon Flats. The flats are approximately 180 miles long and seventy miles wide.

Mile 86.5   There is a scenic overlook at a former quarry to the west. Several tors are visible in the hills to the northeast. This is another good picture-taking spot.

Mile 88   Caribou Mountain (3,200 feet) can be seen to the northwest. Caribou Mountain—one of several peaks with this name in Alaska—was named by D. L. Raeburn, a U.S. Geological Survey employee, in 1901.

Mile 88.5   The highway crosses the summit of Mackey Hill.

Mile 90.2   There are pulloffs to the east and west. The eastern pulloff has a trash barrel. The pipeline can be seen to the north. From late July through mid-August, blueberry-picking is incredible throughout this whole area. The small pink flowers seen along both sides of the highway during this same time of year are almost all from blueberry bushes. If you get a chance to stop and pick a few blueberries, do it! The exquisite taste of Dalton Highway blueberries makes the trip worthwhile in itself.

Mile 94.1   There is a pulloff to the east. The pipeline can be seen to the east. Notice the zig-zag pattern of the pipeline through this area. (See *Introduction*.)

Mile 94   Whimbrel Hill can be seen to the west.

Mile 95   The highway passes above the 2,500-foot line into alpine tundra. If you've never been above treeline before, this is a sight to behold. The absence of trees allows you to see the glorious colors of the alpine tundra shrubs, bushes, and wildflowers—especially from late July through the end of August, when the colors are brightest. This is another place that you don't want to leave without pictures.

Mile 97.5   Finger Rock can be seen to the east as the highway approaches the summit of Finger Mountain. Olson Lake and the Little Kanuti Flats can be seen to the north, and Old Man Camp and Airfield can be seen on the far side of the Kanuti Flats. Finger Rock, named for its finger-like appearance, is the most well-known tor along the highway, and was used as a navigational landmark by early aviators. Several tors can be seen in the next few miles. One of these tors is located a few tenths of a mile past Finger Rock and sits right next to the highway to the east. You can stop here and climb on this tor to get a better view of the valley, or just to say you climbed a tor if you'd like. This stretch of highway atop Finger Mountain is what I believe to be the most breathtaking the road has to offer. As fall approaches in late July and early August, the alpine tundra explodes with the reds, oranges, and yellows of tundra shrubs and wildflowers, which can be enjoyed more fully without the overshadowing presence of trees. If I could spend a week anywhere on the Dalton, I would spend it here on the first week of August. Take the time to enjoy this place before driving on.

Mile 98   Caribou Mountain can be seen very well to the west here.

Mile 100.6 The pipeline passes under the highway. The road that cuts across here follows the pipeline's underground path.

Mile 101   The pipeline becomes visible again to the west, and you can see the zig-zag pattern again as you round the bend.

Mile 102.6 A pipeline access road and buildings are seen to the west.

Mile 102.8 Another pipeline access road and more buildings are seen to the west.

Mile 103.3 The pipeline passes underground.

Mile 105.8 The pipeline emerges from the ground to the west. The highway crosses the Kanuti River. There is a pulloff to the east on the south side of the river. The large container on the west side of the river holds containment equipment for oil emergencies. The word "Kanuti" (also spelled "Konootena") comes from the Koyukon Indian word meaning "Old Man's River." The Kanuti River was often called "Old Man River" by area

Finger Mountain offers spectacular views from its lichen-covered tors. The area is a high point for many visitors including the author. In late season the blueberries are plentiful and delicious.

prospectors around the turn of the century. The Kanuti River flows through the Kanuti National Wildlife Refuge and joins the Koyukuk River about eighty miles downstream from this point. Arctic grayling, burbot, white-fish, and northern pike are all present. The Kanuti River bridge is a popular put-in spot for experienced boaters—this is a difficult river to float—who usually take out at the confluence of the Kanuti and Koyukuk rivers downstream. Note, however, that the take-out point is not accessible by car. Boaters who take this trip have to be picked up by an airplane.

Mile 107   The highway passes the entrance to Old Man Camp to the west. Like Sand Hill, Old Man Camp is built on a sandy dome.

Mile 108.3 The buried pipeline passes under the highway. The pipeline lies under the cleared path you see at this point, and it emerges from the ground to the northeast.

Mile 109.1 There is a pulloff to the west.

Mile 109.7 There is a pulloff to the west.

Mile 109.8 The highway ascends a hill known as the "Beaver Slide." The hill received this name because it is very steep and extremely slippery and muddy when wet. There is a pulloff to the east at the top of the hill.

Mile 110.7 The highway descends the Beaver Slide. Be careful picking up speed on this steep grade.

Mile 111   The area to the west of this point burned in 1990. Watch for black bears in this area during blueberry season—late July, early August. The long-stemmed, multi-flowered, red plants in this area during the same season are fireweed. According to locals, when the top flowers on these long stems finally open, there are exactly six weeks left until the first snowfall.

Mile 112.3 The pipeline access road to the east crosses the original Hickel Highway and the South Fork Fish Creek east of here.

Mile 114   The highway crosses Fish Creek. There is a pulloff to the east on the north side of the creek. Arctic grayling are abundant in the creek.

Recreational gold-panning is allowed within one mile upstream and downstream of the Fish Creek crossing. The original Hickel Highway crossed the present Dalton Highway just north of this point.

Mile 115.3 The highway passes the Arctic Circle (north latitude 66 degrees 33 minutes). This is the point at which the sun does not set for one day at summer solstice, June 20 or 21, and does not rise for one day at winter solstice, December 21 or 22. However, note that you cannot see the midnight sun at summer solstice because hills block your view to the north at this point. See Mile 132 for information on observing the midnight sun. The Arctic Circle sign, at the top of the hill about 0.5 mile to the east, is another popular picture-taking spot. This is also a popular spot for hiking, picnicking, and sightseeing. There are picnic tables and a grill available at the top of the hill, and toilet facilities are nearby. There is an undeveloped campground a few tenths of a mile north of the picnic area. Follow the road east at the top of the hill. If you are traveling with a tour group, you will probably get a certificate at this point stating that you have crossed the Arctic Circle. If you are driving yourself or if you want a personalized certificate, you can order one from the Dalton Highway Survivor's Club, a Fairbanks-based organization. For more information on the club or to order a certificate, write to: The Dalton Highway Survivor's Club, P.O. Box 80649, Fairbanks, Alaska, 99708-0649.

Mile 118 A couple of large tors can be seen on the peak to the northeast. The valley you see to the west is the Koyukuk Basin.

Mile 120.7 The pipeline can be seen to the east.

Mile 124.7 The highway crosses South Fork Bonanza Creek. There is a pulloff with room for a few campsites to the east on the south side of the creek. Tors can be seen on the hilltops on both sides of the highway at this point. Arctic grayling, burbot, and whitefish are all here. Recreational gold-panning is allowed upstream and downstream of the Bonanza Creek crossing, except for the pipeline right-of-way. This area is also a popular spot for hiking.

Mile 125.8 The highway crosses North Fork Bonanza Creek. There are pulloffs to the east on the north and south sides of the creek. Arctic grayling, burbot, and whitefish are in this creek, and recreational gold-panning is allowed downstream and for 2.5 miles upstream of the highway crossing.

Mile 126.5 Tors and other rock outcroppings can be seen on the hilltops on both sides of the highway. These can be difficult to see through the thick trees. Look closely—unless you're driving, of course.

Mile 127.8 There is a small camping area to the west.

Mile 128.9 The pipeline can be seen to the east.

Mile 131.5 Pump Station No. 5 can be seen to the north.

Mile 132 The highway crests Gobbler's Knob (1,500 feet). This hill got its name because it supposedly looks like the head of a turkey from points on the highway farther north. See if you agree. Personally I have never seen the resemblance. This spot is also called "Solstice Point." Because hills block the view at the Arctic Circle (Mile 115.3), this is the southernmost point at which you can watch the sun not set at summer solstice. And this is truly a spectacular sight. If you have some skills with a camera and a little patience, you can make a single photograph of the sun as it drops low in the sky, skirts the horizon, and then climbs back up again—without setting. At this point you have about a seven-day period in which you can see this spectacle. If there is any way you can time your Dalton Highway visit to watch the midnight sun from Solstice Point, do it. I promise you'll never forget the experience. There is a pulloff to the west at this point. The pulloff has trash barrels and toilet facilities and overlooks the Jim River and Prospect Creek. Prospect Creek Camp, Pump Station No. 5, and the airport can be seen to the north. The peaks of the Brooks Range can be seen on the northern horizon.

Mile 135.2 The highway crosses Prospect Creek. The creek was named by prospectors around the turn of the century. Arctic grayling, northern pike, whitefish, and salmon are here. Remember to throw back any salmon caught in the hunting and fishing corridor (see *Recreation*). Recreational gold-panning is allowed downstream and for 1.5 miles upstream of the highway crossing—except for the pipeline right-of-way.

Mile 135.7 There is a pulloff to the west. The Prospect Creek access road leads to the west at this point, and there is an undeveloped campsite next to the Jim River, so named by prospectors, one mile up the access road. Vehicles are allowed on the access road. Recreational gold-panning is allowed for two miles downstream of the end of the access road. This area is also a popular spot for fishing, float boating, picnicking, and sightseeing. The Bettles winter road crosses the river at this point. The winter road is still used to get to and from Bettles when the soil is frozen, but it is closed—and impassable—in the summer. The town is accessible during the summer only by airplane. The town of Bettles was established in 1900 by Gordon C. Bettles, who set up a trading post about six miles down the Middle Fork Koyukuk River from the town's current location. During the gold rush, large riverboats made their way as far as the trading post, where their cargo was transferred to smaller horse-drawn barges to be taken further upstream.

Mile 137.1 The highway passes the entrance to Pump Station No. 5 and a state-operated airport to the east. This pump station, like Pump Station No. 6, was built on a refrigerated foundation so the underlying permafrost would not be thawed.

Mile 138.1 The highway passes the entrance to the Jim River Alaska Department of Transportation and Public Facilities (DOT/PF) maintenance camp to the west.

Mile 140.1 The highway crosses the first of three Jim River crossings. There is a pulloff to the east on the south side of the river. The Jim River is probably the best stream in the region for anglers, and contains arctic grayling, burbot, whitefish, and northern pike. Salmon also migrate through the river. Remember to release any salmon you catch. All three Jim River crossings are popular with boaters, who put in at one of the three bridges and usually take out at the Prospect Creek access road (Mile 135.7 above).

Mile 141 The highway crosses the second Jim River crossing. There is a pulloff to the east on the north side of the river.

Mile 141.8 The highway crosses Douglas Creek.

Mile 144 There is a pulloff to the east.

Mile 144.1 The highway crosses the third Jim River crossing. This is the largest of the three Jim River crossings. There is a pulloff to the east on the south side of the river.

Mile 145.2 The pipeline passes under the highway.

Mile 145.6 The pipeline passes under the highway again.

Mile 150.3 The highway passes Grayling Lake to the east. Grayling Lake is excellent moose habitat, and also provides excellent fishing for arctic grayling. The U-shaped valley you are driving through is typical of the glacially carved valleys beginning here and continuing to the north.

Mile 150.8 There is a pulloff to the east on the north end of Grayling Lake. This pulloff leads to a spot on the lake that is occasionally used for launching fishing boats.

Mile 155.2 There is a pulloff for viewing the South Fork Koyukuk River valley to the west. If you like panoramic shots, this can be a great place for picture-taking.

Mile 156.1 The highway crosses the South Fork Koyukuk River. There are pulloffs to the east and west on the south side of the river, and the river can be accessed via the west pulloff. If you use the west pulloff, please move your automobile so that it does not block access to the river. "Koyukuk" comes from the Koyukon Indian village of Koyukuk (also spelled "Kuyukak" and "Coyukuk"). The Russians that explored this region called the river "Kuiuk" or "Kuyaak." Arctic grayling, whitefish, and salmon can be found within walking distance upstream or downstream of the bridge. Recreational gold-panning is allowed for 1.5 miles upstream and two miles downstream of the highway crossing, except for the pipeline right-of-way. Hiking and float boating are also popular here. The South Fork Koyukuk is a tributary of the Koyukuk River, which flows past the villages of Bettles, Allakaket, Alatna, Hughes, and Huslia before draining into the Yukon River near the village of Koyukuk. This is the point where the north and south legs of the original Haul Road were connected on September 27, 1974.

Mile 157.8 There is a gravel quarry to the east.

Mile 159.1 The pipeline passes under the highway.

Mile 160.5 Chapman Lake and two smaller lakes can be seen to the west as you cross this peak. The Chapman Lake area is excellent for hiking and picnicking.

Mile 161 The road to the west leads to the Tramway Bar. Gold was discovered at Tramway in 1893. The Tramway Bar is actually a canyon along the Middle Fork Koyukuk River. It was first called "Tramway" in 1899, possibly for mining tramways, the small dump carts that run on overhead cables, that may have been used at the mining operations. The Tramway Bar is not well-used because it is located four miles from the highway and because the road is impassable in summer. But if you're willing to walk, it is a good place for fishing and picnicking.

Mile 163.3 There is a pulloff to the west.

Mile 164.5 The Middle Fork of the Koyukuk River runs parallel to the highway to the west beginning at this point and continuing to the Dietrich River crossing (Mile 207.6). Recreational gold-panning is allowed downriver of this location. The Middle Fork Koyukuk is called a braided river because the riverbed can shift and move, changing position when the water is running high.

Mile 164.8 Several sag-bend game crossings (see *Introduction*) can be seen to the east.

Mile 165 The highway passes Cathedral Lake and Cathedral Mountain to the east. These descriptive names were given by prospectors.

Mile 165.1 There is a pulloff to the west.

Mile 165.7 There is a pulloff to the west. This is another popular picture-taking spot.

Mile 166.6 The pipeline passes under the highway.

Mile 169.8 The highway crosses Rosie Creek. This name was first reported in 1932 by Robert Marshall (see *History* for more on Marshall). This creek has also been called Rose Creek and Rosy Creek.

Mile 171.5 Watch for landslides high on the hillsides in this area. These slides are typical of glacially formed valleys. These landslides are high in the mountains and are not a hazard to travelers.

Mile 171.7 There is a large, unnamed lake to the east.

Mile 172.7 There is a private road leading to the east.

Mile 175 The highway passes Coldfoot and the Alaska Department of Transportation and Public Facilities Maintenance Station. There is an airstrip to the west on the north end of Coldfoot, and there is a camping area along the airstrip access road. Emma Dome (5,700 feet) can be seen to the west. Emma Dome was named by August L. Tobin, an area prospector from 1897 to 1918. Tobin named the dome for his wife, Emma L. Tobin. Robert Marshall first reported the name in 1930. Coldfoot has telephone and postal service. The Coldfoot Commercial Complex is the last stop for food, gas, laundry, vehicle repair, lodging, and RV hookups until you arrive at Prudhoe Bay, 239 miles to the north. Coldfoot, originally named "Slate Creek" for its location at the mouth of that creek, was founded in 1899 as a mining camp when prospectors discovered gold on Slate, Myrtle, Clara, Emma, Gold, Porcupine, and other nearby creeks. Its name was reportedly changed to "Coldfoot" when many early prospectors got cold feet as the first winter set in and left the area. Those who stayed were rewarded, however, with new gold strikes along these tributaries of the Middle Fork Koyukuk River. According to Robert Marshall, in 1902 Coldfoot consisted of "one gambling hole, two roadhouses, two stores, and seven saloons." Coldfoot is still used as a base for placer mining operations in many creeks to the north. The BLM, the National Park Service, and the U.S. Fish and Wildlife Service offer displays and evening presentations at their tri-agency visitor information center in town. The original Slate Creek cemetery and a number of mining cabins still exist. The cabins are private property. Dolly Varden, arctic grayling, whitefish, and salmon (remember to release salmon) are all found in Slate Creek as it passes Coldfoot and enters the

Middle Fork Koyukuk River. This is a popular put-in spot for boaters, who usually take out at Bettles. But remember, Bettles is not accessible by car in the summer. The area from Coldfoot to Marion Creek (Mile 179.9) is excellent for such activities as camping, fishing, hiking, picnicking, sightseeing, and even dog-mushing.

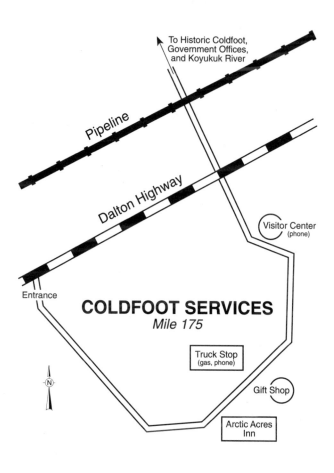

Mile 175.1 The highway crosses Slate Creek. Recreational gold-panning is allowed from 0.25 to 0.75 miles upstream from the Slate Creek crossing. This area has several active claims; make sure you have contacted the BLM for gold-panning instructions before panning in this area.

Mile 176 The highway crosses Clara Creek. This name of local origin was first reported in 1930 by Robert Marshall. Recreational gold-panning is allowed to 0.5 miles upstream of the Clara Creek crossing. Watch for landslides high in the mountains of this valley.

Mile 178.8 There is a small turnoff and a pipeline service building to the west.

Mile 179.8 The Marion Creek campground turnoff is to the east. Parking and camping are available at the campground.

Mile 179.9 The highway crosses Marion Creek.

Mile 180.5 There is a small turnoff to the west.

Mile 183.1 There are several turnoffs with just enough room for one car to the east and west.

Mile 185.9 There is a private road to the east.

Mile 186 There is a pulloff area in a quarry to the east. The mining community of Wiseman can be seen across the Middle Fork Koyukuk River to the west.

Mile 186.7 There are pulloffs to the east and west.

Mile 186.9 There is a private road to the west.

Mile 187.2 The highway crosses Minnie Creek. There are pulloffs to the west on both the north and south sides of the creek. Arctic grayling, burbot, and whitefish are in this small stream. Recreational gold-panning is allowed for 1.5 miles upstream of the highway crossing.

Mile 188.6 The road crosses the first of four Middle Fork Koyukuk River crossings. There is a pulloff to the west on the north side of the river. Arctic grayling, Dolly Varden, whitefish, and salmon are present at all four Middle Fork Koyukuk crossings. The Dalton Highway passes the Wiseman Road, leading to the historic mining community of Wiseman, on the west just north of the river crossing. The road is in fair condition. At times in the past there has been a bed-and-breakfast operating in Wiseman. Contact the Wiseman Trading Co. in town for more information. Wiseman sprung up in 1908 as a supply depot for mining on the Wiseman and Nolan creeks and the Hammond River. Wiseman was originally called "Wright's" for B. E. Wright, keeper of the roadhouse where supplies coming up the Middle Fork Koyukuk River were received. The town's name was changed to "Nolan," after one of the nearby creeks, and then to "Wiseman," after Wiseman

The sign says it all. Wiseman is a community of self-reliant residents and they treasure their independence.

Creek. Robert Marshall used Wiseman as a base for his treks into the Brooks Range and surrounding areas. If you visit Wiseman, respect the property of the few year-round residents. Visit the Wiseman general store, which gives Wiseman a little bit of the feel of a turn-of-the-century gold rush town.

Mile 190.5 The highway crosses the Hammond River. Recreational gold-panning is allowed one mile upstream of the confluence of the river with the Middle Fork Koyukuk.

Mile 190.9 The highway crosses the second Middle Fork Koyukuk River crossing. A pipeline bridge, which supports the pipeline over the river, can be seen to the west.

Mile 193.3 Sukakpak Mountain (4,459 feet) can be seen east of the highway to the north for the first time. "Sukakpak" is an Eskimo word meaning "martin deadfall." Wiehl Mountain (5,765 feet) is east of Sukakpak. Dillon Mountain sits across the valley from Sukakpak and Wiehl. Dillon Mountain was named in honor of Dr. John Thomas Dillon. Dillon was a ten-year veteran of the Alaska Division of Geological and Geophysical Surveys and an affiliate professor of geology at the University of Alaska Fairbanks. Dillon fell in love with the Brooks Range and spent most of his career in Alaska studying it. He went down in his plane as he was returning to Fairbanks from the range after the 1987 field season.

Mile 195 There are several private roads to the east for the next couple of miles.

Mile 197 The highway crosses Gold Creek. The creek was named by area prospectors around the turn of the century. There is an active mine to the east of the highway. This is an excellent hiking and sightseeing spot, but respect the claim rights at the mine and don't trespass.

Mile 197.1 There is a small pulloff to the east.

Mile 197.3 There is a pipeline access road to the west. There is a pulloff to the east.

Mile 197.5 The highway crosses Linda Creek.

Mile 197.7 There is a pulloff on the east side of the highway. Wiehl Mountain can be seen to the east.

Mile 203.5 There is a pulloff with a small footpath leading to the base of Sukakpak Mountain to the east. Ice-cored mounds can often be seen near the base of the mountain. Also watch for landslides on the slopes of Sukakpak and other surrounding mountains.

Mile 204.1 There is a pulloff to the west. This is a good spot for picnics.

Mile 204.3 The highway crosses the third Middle Fork Koyukuk River crossing. This crossing has the best pulloff of the four Middle Fork Koyukuk crossings, with trash barrels and toilet facilities to the east on the north side of the river. This crossing and the next (Mile 204.5) are popular put-in spots with boaters, who take out at either Coldfoot or Bettles.

Mile 204.5 The highway crosses the fourth Middle Fork Koyukuk River crossing.

Mile 205 Snowden Mountain (6,420 feet) is the large mountain to the northeast. Watch for landslides on the high slopes of this mountain. Snowden Mountain was named for Snowden Creek, which heads on its slopes. Snowden Creek was named in 1939 by Robert Marshall for his Eskimo hunting partner, Harry Snowden (see Mile 227.3).

Mile 205.3 There is a pulloff to the west.

Mile 207 The highway crosses the Dietrich River. There is a pulloff to the west on the south side of the river. The Dietrich and Bettles rivers combine at this point to form the Middle Fork Koyukuk River. The Dietrich River runs parallel to the highway to the west for several miles, and the Bettles River disappears to the southeast. The Dietrich River can be reached by foot at several locations over the next twenty-five miles. Dolly Varden, arctic grayling, burbot, and whitefish are present. Recreational gold-panning is allowed on the Bettles River for two miles upstream of the highway crossing. Hiking and float boating are also popular in this area.

Mile 209.3 The highway passes the entrance to Dietrich Camp to the west. The Dietrich Camp airport can be seen to the west.

Mile 210.5 The highway crosses Disaster Creek.

Mile 210.8 There is a pulloff to the east.

Mile 214.2 The highway crosses three unnamed creeks in rapid succession.

Mile 215 The highway passes the Arctic Loon Ponds to the west. Watch for loons in this area.

Mile 219.9 The highway crosses an unnamed creek.

Mile 221.1 The highway crosses another unnamed creek.

Mile 221.8 There is a pulloff to the east.

Mile 223 Watch for landslides on the upper slopes of the hills to the east.

Mile 226 There is a pipeline communication building to the west.

Mile 227.3 The highway crosses Nutirwik Creek. The structures that can be seen on the east side of the highway protect the buried pipe. This is a popular hiking area. Nutirwik Creek was named in 1939 by Robert Marshall for his Eskimo hunting partner, Harry Snowden. Snowden's Eskimo name was "Nutirwik."

Mile 231.2 There are pulloffs to the east and west.

Mile 234.1 The highway passes the southern boundary of the North Slope Borough.

Mile 235 The highway passes the northernmost white spruce along the pipeline route. This tree can be seen on the east side of the highway. Look for a descriptive sign at the base of the tree. This is the northern limit of treeline along the Dalton Highway. For the next 180 miles to the Arctic Ocean, the climate is too harsh for most trees to survive. You won't see many sights like this anywhere else. A picture is a must. In the pulloff areas, you can see lots of slate with quartz veins running through it.

Mile 235.3 There is a pulloff with a trash barrel to the west. The highway passes the base of the Chandalar Shelf and begins a long, steep—nine percent—grade to the top of the shelf. The view of the Chandalar is another awe-inspiring sight. This is a great spot for a picture. The Chandalar Shelf was named for the Chandalar River (Mile 244.6).

Mile 237.1 The highway crests the Chandalar Shelf. There is a pulloff to the west. Table Mountain (6,314 feet) can be seen to the southeast. This is an excellent location for hiking and sightseeing.

Mile 239.2 The highway passes the entrance to Chandalar Camp to the east. This camp is now used as a BLM field station. Be especially careful of bears in this area.

Mile 239.4 The highway passes the Chandalar highway maintenance station to the west. There is an airstrip to the east.

Mile 240.3 The pipeline emerges from the ground to the northeast.

Mile 244.6 The highway crosses the west fork of the North Fork Chandalar River. The name "Chandalar" comes from employees of the Hudson's Bay Company at Fort Yukon in the mid- to late-1800s. The French employees of the company called the Gwich'in Indians of the area "Gens de Large," meaning "nomadic people." "Gens de Large" evolved into "Chandalar" when it was written in English. (If you sound out "Gens de Large" you can hear the similarity to "Chandalar.")

Mile 244.7 The highway begins the climb towards Atigun Pass. The pass can be seen to the north. This is another great picture-taking spot. Pull your car well off the road if you stop here. And watch for trucks coming off the pass. You are driving into the heart of the Brooks Range. The range was named in 1925 by the U.S. Geological Survey for Alfred Hulse Brooks. Brooks was the chief Alaska geologist for the Geological Survey from 1903 to 1924.

Mile 246.8 The highway crests Atigun Pass and the Continental Divide (4,800 feet). This is the highest highway summit in Alaska. Watch for Dall sheep as you crest the pass and descend the north side of the summit. The National Weather Service maintains a remote weather station that can be seen to the east of the summit. There is a pulloff to the east at the summit, but be very cautious about stopping here. Atigun Pass is the most nerve-racking stretch of the Dalton Highway for truckers, and the last thing they want to see is a car sticking into the road at the summit. If you want to stop, make sure you are well off the road. And it would be much appreciated if you stopped here only when you have a few minutes without any truck traffic. The mountains west of the highway at this point are the Endicott Mountains. These mountains were named in 1885 for William Crowninshield Endicott, who served as Secretary of War under President Grover Cleveland.

Mile 246.9 The highway begins the steep descent into Atigun Valley. Atigun Valley is another of the glacially carved valleys typical of the Dalton Highway region. The pipeline passes under the highway.

Mile 247 The stakes in the valley throughout this area mark the path of the buried pipeline. This is one of the areas where the pipeline was buried in permafrost-rich soil (see *Introduction*) because of outside dangers—in this case, avalanches, which are common through this area in winter.

Mile 247.3 The Atigun River runs parallel to the highway to the east at this point.

Mile 248.4 There are pulloffs to the east and west.

Mile 249.5 The highway crosses Spike Camp Creek. Watch for Northern wheatears in this area. These robin-sized birds are as thick as flies in this area at some points during the summer.

Mile 250 The highway passes the entrance to Atigun Camp to the east. There are pulloffs to the east and west. James Dalton Mountain (7,010 feet) can be seen directly northwest of Atigun Camp. This peak is a further tribute to the man for whom the highway is named.

Mile 252.7 The highway crosses several unnamed creeks.

Mile 253 The highway crosses the first Atigun River crossing. There is a small turnout to the east on the south side of the river. The pipeline passes under the highway. Several miles of the Atigun River can be reached by foot between here and the next crossing (Mile 270.8). Arctic grayling, Dolly

Looking south from near the crest of Atigun Pass, the dust that signals approaching vehicles is evident. Here the pipeline is buried to protect it from the avalanches and landslides of the pass.

Varden, burbot, and whitefish are all present in this section of the Atigun River. Fly-fishing is especially popular from here north during the summer.

Mile 255.1 There is a pipeline access road and building to the west.

Mile 255.4 The pipeline emerges from underground to the west.

Mile 257 A valve on the pipeline can be seen to the west.

Mile 258.5 The highway crosses Trevor Creek.

Mile 260.7 There is a pulloff to the east. This pulloff is part of a pipeline access road that leads further to the east.

Mile 263.5 There is a pulloff to the east. Notice all of the rock slides on the slopes of the mountains to the east in this area. These are more fingerprints of past glaciers in the area.

Mile 265.1 The highway crosses Roche Moutonnée Creek. A "roche moutonnée" is a small, rounded hill made of bedrock that has been glacially carved. Several of these hillocks exist in the Brooks Range.

Mile 267 Pump Station No. 4 can be seen to the north.

Mile 267.5 The highway crosses an unnamed creek.

Mile 269.2 The highway passes the entrance to Pump Station No. 4. This pump station is operated on natural gas.

Mile 269.4 The pipeline passes under the highway. A lake can be seen to the west.

Mile 270 Tea Lake can be seen to the west. It can be reached by a short downhill walk. Arctic grayling, burbot, and lake trout are all present.

Mile 270.8 The highway crosses the second Atigun River crossing. From this point the Atigun River flows east through the Atigun Gorge to the Sagavanirktok River. The western boundary of the Arctic National Wildlife Refuge is located three miles to the east in the gorge. Galbraith Lake can be seen to the west.

Near Pump Station No. 4, the trans-Alaska pipeline passes through a U-shaped glacial valley common in the Brooks Range.

Mile 271.7 A small lake can be seen to the west.

Mile 272.5 Galbraith Lake can be seen to the west for the next couple of miles. The Galbraith Lake construction camp and airport are located to the west of the lake. Galbraith Lake was named by the U.S. Geological Survey in 1951 in honor of Bart Galbraith, a bush pilot who went down while flying in this area. The Eskimo name for the lake is "Natravak," or "big lake."

Mile 274.7 The highway passes an access road to the Galbraith Lake airstrip to the west. The access road crosses an inlet stream about 1.5 miles above the lake. The 1.5 miles from the access road to the lake must be hiked. Few visitors want to make such a hike, so Galbraith Lake is lightly fished. However, arctic grayling, Dolly Varden, lake trout, burbot, and whitefish are all present in the lake. The area around Galbraith Lake is excellent for hiking, picnicking, and sightseeing. Two unnamed Brooks Range glaciers can be seen to the south at this point. If you wish to see them, you need to drive down the access road to a point near the airstrip entrance. I highly recommend making this short side trip. These are the only glaciers visible from the Dalton Highway.

Mile 276   Island Lake can be seen to the west. It is a short walk from the highway to Island Lake, and the lake is populated by arctic char, arctic grayling, lake trout, and whitefish. Anglers occasionally land twenty- to twenty-two-pound lake trout at Island Lake.

Mile 282   Toolik Lake can first be seen to the north. "Toolik," or "tulilik," is an Eskimo word meaning "king loon." Toolik Lake, along with several other small lakes in this area, has resident populations of arctic grayling, lake trout, and whitefish. This is an excellent area for hiking and sightseeing.

Mile 284.2   The highway passes the entrance to Toolik construction camp. Toolik Lake can be seen to the west. There is a marked access road to the lake. The access road also leads to the University of Alaska Biology Field Research Station, where scientists study the vegetation, soils, streams, and lakes in the region. The research station is not open to the public. There is also an airstrip at the camp.

Mile 284.7   Travelers pass the Toolik area sign. Caribou often congregate in this area in mid-August. If you pass through at this time, watch for them.

Mile 286.1   There is a pulloff with a litter barrel to the east. This high point in the highway is a great place to look back at the Brooks Range and a place to get some good pictures.

Mile 287   Horizon Lake can be seen east of the highway.

Mile 288.9   The highway crosses the Kuparuk River. There are pulloffs to the east on the north and south sides of the river. "Kuparuk," or "Koopowra," is an Eskimo word first recorded by prospector S. J. Marsh in 1901. He interpreted it to mean "big river."

Mile 289.2   The pipeline passes under the highway.

Mile 290.3 There is a pulloff to the east. Directly after the pulloff there is an access road to a pipeline material site.

Mile 297.9 The highway crosses Oksrukuyik Creek. "Oksrukuyik" is an Eskimo word, although I haven't found a translation yet. There is a pulloff to the east on the south side of the creek. Arctic grayling and burbot are both present in the creek.

Mile 298.3 The highway crests a large hill. The Sagavanirktok River—or "Sag River," as it is commonly called—valley can be seen to the north. The mountains east of the river are the Philip Smith Mountains. The Philip Smith Mountains were named in 1950 by the U.S. Geological Survey for Philip Sidney Smith, chief Alaska geologist of the Survey from 1925 to 1946. He was also the director of the Geological Survey for a time.

Mile 302 Slope Mountain (4,010 feet) can be seen to the west. This is the northern terminus of the BLM-managed lands of the Utility Corridor. Land north of this point is owned and managed by the State of Alaska. Ice-cored mounds can often be seen near the pipeline to the west. Watch for both Dall sheep and raptors on Slope Mountain. The area around the mountain is excellent for hiking and sightseeing.

Mile 305.4 The highway passes the Sag River Camp of the Alaska Department of Transportation, formerly the Slope Mountain Construction Camp, to the east.

Mile 308.8 The Sagavanirktok River can be seen close to the highway to the east. "Sagavanirktok," also spelled "Shagavanuktok," comes from the Eskimo word "Sawanutko," meaning "strong current." The name was first recorded by prospector S. J. Marsh in 1901. From this point north the Sag River runs parallel to the highway. The river can be reached from the highway at several points, including Mile 313 (just north of Pump Station No. 3), Mile 325 (Ice Cut), and Mile 334 (near the Happy Valley airstrip). Arctic grayling, burbot, Dolly Varden, and whitefish are all present.

Mile 309 Pump Station No. 3 can be seen to the north.

Mile 311.9 The highway passes the entrance to Pump Station No. 3. This pump station was also constructed with a refrigerated foundation to prevent melting the underlying permafrost. Ice-cored mounds can sometimes be seen to the north of the station on the west side of the highway. There is a pipeline access road to the east.

Mile 312 The Kakuktukruich Bluff (2,000 feet) can be seen to the east of the highway.

Mile 314.9 A small, unnamed lake can be seen to the east.

Mile 317.9 The highway crosses an unnamed creek.

Mile 319.8 Travelers descend Oil Spill Hill. There is a pulloff to the east. Although the name of this hill has obvious connotations, I have been unable to verify that there was ever an oil spill here.

Mile 324.9 The highway ascends steeply out of the Sag River valley to a ridge of cliffs called "Ice Cut." There is a pulloff and a comfortable camping area at the base of Ice Cut. Another pulloff with a trash barrel is on the east side at the top of the ridge. Several raptors nest in these cliffs. This is an excellent spot for picnicking and sightseeing.

Mile 326.3 The pipeline passes under the highway.

Mile 330.8 The highway crosses Dan Creek. Parking for three or four cars is available on the west shoulder of the highway near the crossing. The creek contains arctic grayling.

Mile 334.2 The highway crosses Happy Valley Creek. There are turnouts to the east and west on the north side of the creek. Arctic grayling are present in the creek. Ice-wedge polygons can sometimes be seen on both sides of the highway in this area. Exposed ice wedges can also occasionally be seen. Happy Valley Creek flows into the Sag River at the north end of the Happy Valley airstrip to the west. The Sag River is popular with experienced boaters—this is a Class IV river—who put in and take out all along the river from this point north.

Mile 334.4 The highway passes the entrance to Happy Valley construction camp—now an airstrip—to the east. This area is now under private lease. Do not trespass. There is an excellent camping spot to the west.

Mile 334.5 The highway crosses an unnamed creek. This creek—and several the highway crosses in this area—feeds the Sag River.

Mile 337 Look for polygons in this area.

Mile 338.6 The highway crosses another creek that feeds the Sag River.

Mile 344.1 There is a pipeline equipment and supply site near the highway.

Mile 350 The highway begins its ascent into the Sagwon Uplands. The Sagwon Bluffs can be seen to the north. Raptors make their homes in the bluffs. Also watch for musk ox in this area. This is another excellent area for hiking and sightseeing.

Mile 354 The Arctic Coastal Plain (North Slope) begins.

Mile 358.8 The highway passes the entrance to Pump Station No. 2. Tall reflectors on either side of the highway beginning at this point guide travelers to Deadhorse. These reflectors are a real lifesaver in winter. When the snow blows and drifts, the highway disappears in this flat terrain. I drove to Deadhorse one February night during a windstorm and—except for the reflectors—had no idea where the highway was. Such are the unique dangers of the Dalton. Once in a while, snowy owls will perch on these reflectors. Keep an eye out for them.

Mile 363.7 Ice-cored mounds can often be seen to the west at this point.

Mile 365.1 There is a pulloff with a trash barrel to the west.

Mile 367.8 A thaw lake can be seen to the west. This is the first of several thaw lakes you will see along the highway from this point north. Few of these lakes are officially named, although several have home-made signs giving them unofficial names.

Mile 371   A large pingo can be seen to the northwest.

Mile 377.5 The highway passes the entrance to Franklin Bluffs construction camp. There is a trash barrel at the former camp site. The Franklin Bluffs begin to the east. Watch for brown bears in this area, particularly near the Sag River.

Mile 380   The stakes to the east mark the path of the buried pipeline in this area.

Mile 385   Two more pingos can be seen far to the west.

Mile 392   Another large pingo and two smaller ones can be seen to the northwest.

Mile 399.8 The pipeline passes under the highway for the last time before heading towards Pump Station No. 1. A pingo can be seen to the west. You should be able to see some polygons to both the east and west at this location.

Mile 401   The highway passes the northern end of the Franklin Bluffs. Watch for caribou and musk ox in this area. During the summer, a fog bank is common between Franklin Bluffs and Prudhoe Bay, particularly in the morning. Drive carefully if you get caught in the fog.

Mile 405   The Prudhoe Bay oil fields can be seen to the north for the first time. Prudhoe Bay is 9.6 miles across and stretches between Heald Point and Point McIntyre on the Beaufort Sea. It was named in 1826 by Sir John Franklin, an English arctic explorer.

Mile 405.4 The highway passes Alexander Lake to the west. Alexander Lake is one of the few named thaw lakes in the region.

Mile 411.1 Travelers enter the "No Hunting" zone. This means just what it says: No Hunting is allowed from this point north.

Mile 414   The highway enters the town of Deadhorse. There is a pingo to the west near the entrance to town. Pump Station No. 1 is just north of town. This is the northern terminus of the Dalton Highway. That's it—you've reached the end of the Dalton! At Deadhorse, follow the marked highway through town to the first stop sign. To the left are Natchiq, Arctic Caribou Inn, a Princess Tours office, and the Commercial Center. To the right are the North Star Inn and the oil fields. To reach the oil field checkpoints, drive past the North Star Inn to the first stop sign. Turn either left or right and follow the road to the end. These two roads lead to the west (controlled by BP Exploration) and east (controlled by ARCO Alaska, Inc.) oil field checkpoints. Remember: you must have clearance to travel on the oil fields. (See *Traveling the Dalton Highway.*)

INDEX OF AGENCIES

Alaska Department of Fish and Game, 1300 College Road, Fairbanks, Alaska, 99701-1599. 907-456-5161.

Alaska Department of Fish and Game, Licensing Section, P.O. Box 25525, Juneau, Alaska, 99802-5525.

Alaska Department of Transportation (road condition recording), Fairbanks, Alaska. 907-456-7623.

Alaska Division of Geological and Geophysical Surveys, 3700 Airport Way, Fairbanks, Alaska, 99709.

Alaska Division of Tourism, P.O. Box 110801, Juneau, AK, 99811-0801.

Alaska Public Lands Information Center, 250 Cushman Street, Suite 1A, Fairbanks, Alaska, 99701. 907-451-7352.

Bureau of Land Management, Arctic District Office, 1150 University Avenue, Fairbanks, AK, 99709-3804. 907-474-2302. Anchorage District Office, 6881 Abbott Loop Road, Anchorage, Alaska, 99513. 907-267-1204.

Department of Commerce and Economic Development, Division of Occupational Licensing, Big Game Commercial Services Board, Box 11806, Juneau, Alaska, 99811-0806. 907-465-2534.

Fairbanks Automated Flight Service Center, Fairbanks, Alaska. 907-474-8395.

Federal Aviation Administration, Anchorage, Alaska. 907-271-5296.

National Weather Service, Fairbanks, Alaska. 907-456-0247.

Refuge Manager, Arctic National Wildlife Refuge, Federal Building and Courthouse, Box 20, 101 12th Street, Fairbanks, Alaska, 99701. 907-456-0250.

Refuge Manager, Kanuti National Wildlife Refuge, Federal Building and Courthouse, Box 20, 101 12th Street, Fairbanks, Alaska, 99701. 907-456-0329.

Refuge Manager, Yukon Flats National Wildlife Refuge, Federal Building and Courthouse, Box 14, 101 12th Street, Fairbanks, Alaska, 99701. 907-456-0440.

Superintendent, Gates of the Arctic National Park and Preserve, P.O. Box 74680, 201 1st Ave., Fairbanks, Alaska, 99707-4680. 907-456-0281.

U.S. Geological Survey, 101 12th Street, Fairbanks, Alaska, 99701. 907-456-0244.

SUGGESTED READING

A Field Guide to Animal Tracks, by Olaus Murie. Published by Houghton Mifflin Company, 1976.

A Guide to the Birds of Alaska, by R. Armstrong. Published by Alaska Northwest Publishing, Seattle, WA, 1980.

A Guide to Wildlife Viewing in Alaska. Published by the Alaska Department of Fish and Game. If you live in Alaska, you can order this guide by calling the Department of Fish and Game at 1-800-478-4286; if you live outside Alaska, call the department *collect* at (907) 465-4286.

Alaska Trees and Shrubs, by Leslie A. Viereck and Elbert L. Little, Jr. Published by the University of Alaska Press, 1986.

Alaska Mammals. Published by the Alaska Geographic Society, 1981.

Alaska Wilderness: Exploring the Central Brooks Range, by Robert Marshall. Published by the University of California Press (Berkeley), 1970.

Arctic Village, by Robert Marshall. Published by the University of Alaska Press, 1991.

Dictionary of Alaska Place Names, by Donald Orth. Published by the Government Printing Office, 1967.

Elliott and Dalton Highways, Fox to Prudhoe Bay, Alaska: Guidebook to Permafrost and Related Features, edited by Jerry Brown and R. A. Kreig. Guidebook 4 of the International Conference on Permafrost, Fairbanks, Alaska, 1983.

Facts about Alaska (The Alaska Almanac), 16th Edition, edited by Carolyn Smith. Published by Alaska Northwest Books, 1992.

Roadside Geology of Alaska, by Cathy Connor and Daniel O'Haire. Published by Mountain Press Publishing Co., Missoula, MT, 1988.

Travels in Alaska, by John Muir. Published by Houghton Mifflin Company, 1979.

**Explore the West with
UMBRELLA BOOKS ®**

CALIFORNIA LIGHTHOUSES, a guide to the more than 40 lighthouse stations marking California's 1,200 miles of coast, by Sharlene & Ted Nelson. $12.95.

BICYCLING THE OREGON COAST, a bicyclist's discovery of the 370-mile route along America's most beautiful coastline, by Robin Cody. $10.95.

NORTHWEST NATURAL HOTSPRINGS, a guide that will make you want to jump into your car or boat and head for the nearest hotspring, by Tom Stockley. $10.95.

INLAND NORTHWEST ANTIQUE STORES, a humorous guide to the best antique stores of central and eastern Washington and north Idaho, by Bill London. $12.95.

INLAND EMPIRE (eastern Washington, northern Idaho), an introduction to many of the colorful residents and local lore in thirteen tours, by Bill London. $10.95.

WASHINGTON LIGHTHOUSES, the only guide available to Washington's 25 lighthouses, by Sharlene & Ted Nelson. $12.95.

PORTS OF CALL OF SOUTHEAST ALASKA, an insider's perspective on the region's independent people and unique places, by Sherry Simpson. $12.95.

ALASKA'S WILDERNESS HIGHWAY, a must companion for those planning to travel over the lonely, remote but beautiful Dalton Highway, by Mike Jensen. $10.95.

OREGON LIGHTHOUSES, a look at the legends associated with 14 lighthouses along the coast and up the Columbia River, by Sharlene & Ted Nelson. $10.95.

GRAND OLD HOTELS OF WASHINGTON & OREGON, an exploration to discover the finest of the region's historic hotels, inns, and lodges, by Christine Ummel. $12.95.

Mail your orders to: Epicenter Press, Box 82368, Kenmore Station, Seattle, WA 98028. Add $2 per book for book-rate shipping. (Washington residents must also add $.90 sales tax for each $10.95 title, $1.06 for each $12.95 title.)

NOTES

NOTES

NOTES

ALEX BOYD

ABOUT THE AUTHOR

Although born and raised in the "Lower 48," Mike Jensen considers himself an Alaskan at heart. He moved to Fairbanks with his wife and two sons—a third son was born in Alaska—partly for a change of pace and partly to complete a master's degree in professional writing at the University of Alaska Fairbanks. While completing his degree, he travelled throughout the state looking for the true "Alaskan experience." He found it on the Dalton Highway.

Mike first wrote *The Umbrella Guide to Alaska's Wilderness Highway* as part of the work for this master's degree. Mike has also published magazine articles on subjects as diverse as religion and computers. He has written several travel and recreation pieces on Alaska, and continues to explore the state whenever he can. In addition to being a husband and a father, Mike likes to spend his winters skiing in Utah and his summers seeking adventure wherever he can find it.